Titanic

*Scenes from the
British Wreck Commissioner's Inquiry
1912*

by

Owen McCafferty

directed by
Charlotte Westenra

GW00503613

A MAC production

Titanic received its first performance
at the MAC on Sunday 22nd April 2012

Titanic

Scenes from
the British Wreck Commissioner's Inquiry 1912

Clerk of the Court (a fictional character)
Ian McElhinney

COUNSEL

The Commissioner, Lord Mersey	**Paul Moriarty**
Attorney General, Sir Rufus Isaacs	**Michael Hadley**
Solicitor General, Sir John Simon	**Ben Caplan**
Mr Thomas Scanlon MP	**Caolan Byrne**
Mr W D Harbinson	**Rufus Wright**

WITNESSES
in order of appearance

Reginald Lee	**Timothy Chipping**
Charles Joughin	**Kevin Trainor**
John Hart	**Jack Beale**
George Symons	**Thomas Howes**
Sir Cosmo Duff Gordon	**Jay Villiers**
Lady Duff Gordon	**Andrea Irvine**
Charles Lightoller	**James Tucker**
Joseph Ismay	**Patrick O' Kane**
Sir Ernest Shackleton	**James Hillier**

Director	**Charlotte Westenra**
Set and Costume Design	**Richard Kent**
Lighting Design	**Conleth White**
Sound Design	**James Kennedy**
Casting Director	**Georgia Simpson**
Executive Producer	**Patrick Talbot**
Production Manager	**Alan McCracken**
Company Stage Manager	**Patrick Freeman**
Deputy Stage Manager	**Cara McGimpsey**
Assistant Stage Manager	**Natalie Murphy**
Wardrobe Supervisor	**Elle Kent**
Assistant Director	**Josh Seymour**
Voice Coach	**Peter Ballance**
Set Construction	**Stage Hand Sets**

Originally commissioned in 2011
by the Ulster Bank Belfast Festival at Queen's
with support from the Arts Council of Northern Ireland and ni 2012

Creative Producer: Graeme Farrow

The MAC

Created at a cost of £18 million, the MAC houses two theatres, three galleries, dance studios and rehearsal rooms, workshop spaces and an artist in residence space as well as a number of multi-purpose spaces and offices for four resident companies. Our performance spaces allow us to develop unique and exciting collaborations with writers, actors, dancers, designers, musicians, directors and theatre makers that will excite, inspire and entertain audiences of all ages from across Northern Ireland and beyond. Our ambition is to be excellent in everything we do and to foster creativity and innovation amongst home-grown artists as well as those from around the world. It is entirely fitting therefore, as well as thrilling, that we open our doors to the public for the first time in April 2012 by bringing a brand new work from one of Ireland's finest writers to the stage.

The opportunity to have Owen McCafferty's work as the inaugural MAC production is a significant event for all concerned. As well as marking the opening of one of Northern Ireland's most momentous cultural spaces, *Titanic (Scenes from the British Wreck Commissioner's Inquiry, 1912)* also forms a major part of the Titanic centenary events in Northern Ireland. Under the skilful direction of Charlotte Westenra, together with a fine company of actors, we believe that Owen's work is perhaps one of the most human Titanic dramas of all and that the words of the survivors present a compelling story that will resonate with audiences. Finally, we would like to thank Northern Ireland Tourist Board and Belfast City Council for their generous support in making this production happen.

Gillian Mitchell, Director of Programmes

BIOGRAPHIES

OWEN McCAFFERTY

Born in 1961, Owen McCafferty lives with his wife, three children and granddaughter in Belfast. His work for stage includes SHOOT THE CROW (Druid, Galway 1997, Royal Exchange Manchester 2003, Prime Cut Productions at Waterfront Studio Belfast 2011 and Grand Opera House Belfast 2012), MOJO, MICKYBO (Kabosh Belfast 1998), CLOSING TIME (National Theatre London 2002), COLD COMFORT (Prime Cut Productions Belfast 2002), SCENES FROM THE BIG PICTURE (National Theatre London 2003), DAYS OF WINE AND ROSES (Donmar Warehouse 2005), a version of Sophocles' ANTIGONE (Prime Cut Productions Belfast 2008) and THE ABSENCE OF WOMEN (Lyric Theatre Belfast and Tricycle Theatre London 2011). He has won the Meyer-Whitworth, John Whiting and Evening Standard Awards for New Playwriting.

CHARLOTTE WESTENRA / Director

Charlotte studied Drama at Manchester University and trained with TIPP (Theatre in Prisons and Probation) and Augusto Boal's Centre of the Theatre of the Oppressed in Rio de Janeiro.

Previous directing work includes: four plays as part of SIXTY-SIX BOOKS (Bush Theatre), CELEBRITY 24 HOUR PLAYS 2010 and 2011 (Old Vic), LOWER NINTH (Donmar at Trafalgar Studios), MY DAD'S A BIRDMAN (Sheffield Crucible), THE OBAMA PROJECT (National Theatre Studio London/ Ingmar Bergman Festival Stockholm), KISS OF THE SPIDER WOMAN (Donmar), DARFUR-HOW LONG IS NEVER? (Tricycle), WHEN FIVE YEARS PASS (Arcola), GLADIATOR GAMES (Studio, Sheffield Crucible & Theatre Royal, Stratford East), FEMALE PARTS (Contact, Manchester), WAITING FOR LEFTY – finalist for 2003 James Menzies Kitchin Award for Young Directors (BAC).

As Associate Director: PIAF, FROST/NIXON (Donmar West End Transfer), BLOODY SUNDAY – SCENES FROM THE SAVILLE INQUIRY (Derry Millennium Theatre, Belfast Opera House & Tricycle) and JUSTIFYING WAR (Tricycle). As Resident Assistant Director at the Donmar: GRAND HOTEL, HECUBA, OLD TIMES, HENRY IV, THE DARK, WORLD MUSIC.

RICHARD KENT / Set and Costume Design

Recent work includes: RICHARD 11 (Donmar Warehouse), MIXED MARRIAGE (Finborough Theatre), THE STRONGER/THE PARIAH (Arcola), DECLINE AND FALL (Old Red Lion), GIN AND TONIC and PASSING TRAINS (Tramway, Glasgow).

Richard has worked as Associate to Christopher Oram since 2008, Working on numerous shows at the Donmar Including SPELLING BEE, KING LEAR (also BAM, New York), PASSION, RED (also Broadway and Mark Taper Forum, LA 2012), A STREETCAR NAMED DESIRE as well as IVANOV, TWELFTH NIGHT, MADAME DE SADE, (Donmar West End) and HAMLET (DWE, Elsinore Denmark and Broadway). Other work as associate includes DON GIOVANNI (Metropolitan Opera), MADAME BUTTERFLY (Houston Grand Opera), BILLY BUDD (Glyndebourne), COMPANY (Sheffield Crucible), DANTON'S DEATH (National Theatre) and the upcoming shows EVITA (Broadway) and NOZZE DI FIGARO (Glyndebourne).

CONLETH WHITE / Lighting Design

Designs include: CARTHAGINIANS at the Millenium Forum Derry and on national tour, THE CHRONICLES OF LONG KESH at the Waterfront Studio and Tricycle Theatre London, LAY UP YOUR ENDS at the Grand Opera House, A NIGHT IN NOVEMBER at the Olympia Theatre Dublin and Trafalgar Studios London. THE COUNTRY GIRLS, Gaiety Theatre Dublin and national tour, WHEN JOLIE MET CHRISTY, THE PARTING GLASS, THE TOWNLANDS OF BRAZIL, all for Axis Dublin, THE LITTLE MERMAID for Big Telly in Belfast, Belgrade, Taiwan, Denmark and the UK.

JAMES KENNEDY / Sound Design

Previous sound designs include: FLY ME TO THE MOON, DANCING SHOES, CHRISTMAS EVE CAN KILL YOU, STORMONT, THE INTERROGATION OF AMBROSE FOGARTY, GUIDELINES FOR A LONG AND HAPPY LIFE, FAMILY PLOT, GIRLS AND DOLLS, DUKE OF HOPE, SLEEP EAT PARTY, THE SIGN OF THE WHALE, RJ'S LEAVING DAY and PROTESTANTS.

GEORGIA SIMPSON / Casting Director

Films include GOOD VIBRATIONS, THE SHORE (winner of 2012 Academy Award for Live Action Short Film), CHERRYBOMB, and FIVE MINUTES OF HEAVEN (winner of Sundance Film Festival World Cinema Directing Award for Oliver Hirschbiegel, and BAFA nominated for Television Single Drama).

TV includes V SIGN, BEST: HIS MOTHER'S SON and MESSIAH.

PATRICK TALBOT / Executive Producer

Patrick Talbot established Patrick Talbot Productions in September 2011. It is a production company, a provider of executive producing services and a tour booker. It has produced THE SUNBEAM GIRLS at the Cork Opera House and INTIMACIES AND ELEPHANTS, based on the writings of Raymond Carver, which was also adapted and directed by Patrick and produced in association with the Everyman Palace Theatre.

As co-director of Green Light Management he produced Irish tours by Julian Lloyd Webber and Sir Tom Courtenay in 2011.

Patrick was Artistic Director/CEO of the Everyman Palace Theatre from 2001 to 2011.

IAN McELHINNEY / Clerk of the Court

TELEVISION includes: TITANIC: BLOOD & STEEL, GAME OF THRONES, NEW TRICKS, BETRAYAL OF TRUST, SCAPEGOAT, RAW, LITTLE DORRIT, CHILDSPLAY, SINGLE HANDED (Series 1 + 2).

FILM includes: THREE WISE WOMEN, CUP CAKE, BITTERSWEET, LEAP YEAR, OCCI VERSUS THE WORLD, SHINE OF RAINBOWS, TRIAGE, CLOSING THE RING, MAPMAKER, BORSTAL BOY, DIVORCING JACK, HIDDEN AGENDA, and HAMLET.

THEATRE includes: A DELICATE BALANCE, THROUGH A GLASS DARKLY, THERE CAME A GYPSY RIDING all at the Almeida Theatre, AMPHIBIANS for the RSC, PYGMIES IN THE RUINS at the Royal Court Theatre, THE CURE AT TROY at the Tricycle Theatre. UNCLE VANYA, THE ABSENCE OF WOMEN, THE HOME PLACE, all at the Lyric Theatre Belfast.

As director includes: STONES IN HIS POCKET by Marie Jones (Belfast, Dublin, London and New York).

PAUL MORIARTY / Lord Mersey

THEATRE includes: TRANSLATIONS at Curve Theatre, NINETEEN EIGHTY FOUR at Manchester Royal Exchange, SUS at the Young Vic, ROSMERSHOLM, RICHARD II,CORIOLANUS all at Almeida Theatre, THE ELEPHANT MAN (National Tour), SAVED at the Abbey Theatre Dublin, A VIEW FROM THE BRIDGE at Sheffield Crucible, SERIOUS MONEY at Wyndhams and New York, MARKET BOY, PILLARS OF THE COMMUNITY, SING YER HEART OUT FOR THE LADS, MACBETH, BLACK SNOW, AS I LAY DYING, THE CRUCIBLE, RACING DEMON, ABSENCE OF WAR all at the National Theatre.

TELEVISION includes: ASHES TO ASHES, HOLBY CITY, JACK OF HEARTS, EASTENDRES, A TOUCH OF FROST, THE KNOCK, MURDER MOST HORRID, PRIDE AND PREJUDICE, WYCLIFFE, and SHINE ON HARVEY MOON.

FILM includes: QUEST FOR LOVE and HIDDEN AGENDA.

MICHAEL HADLEY / Sir Rufus Isaacs

TELEVISION includes: MRS BIGGS, CHURCHILL AT WAR, STRANGE, PARADISE HEIGHTS, ROUGH JUSTICE, THE CATHERINE WHEEL, THE SAMARITANS, QUEEN VICTORIA'S SCANDAL, LIFE OF SHAKESPEARE, THE MARRYING KIND, THE PROFESSIONALS and BROOKSIDE.

FILM includes: THE BOAT THAT ROCKED, UNRELATED, THREE BLIND MICE, THE BEST PAIR OF LEGS IN THE BUSINESS, ALL COPPERS ARE, and THEY RAN BEFORE THE WIND.

THEATRE includes: RICHARD II, KING LEAR, THE VORTEX, LITTLE FOXES at the Donmar, HAMLET on Broadway, PIAF, Donmar/West End, CORIOLANUS, CANTERBURY TALES, RICHARD III, AS YOU LIKE IT at the RSC, DON CARLOS, Sheffield Crucible/West End, THE WOMAN IN BLACK, national tour/West End, and THE JEW OF MALTA at the Almeida.

BEN CAPLAN / Solicitor General, Sir John Simon

FILM includes: LEAP YEAR, ROCKNROLLA.

TELEVISION includes: CALL THE MIDWIFE, WHITECHAPEL 3, DARK MATTERS, THE RUNAWAY, TRINITY, THE PASSION, MAXWELL, THE CANDIDATE, JUDGE JOHN DEED, DWARFS, BAND OF BROTHERS, A TOUCH OF FROST, SOLDIER, SOLDIER, INSPECTOR MORSE, THE PERFECT BLUE and WHERE THE HEART IS.

THEATRE includes: PUSHING UP POPPIES at Theatre 503, SEVEN JEWISH CHILDREN at the Royal Court, THE COMMON PERSUIT at the Chocolate Factory, THREE SISTERS ON HOPE STREET at the Everyman and Hampstead, TWO THOUSAND YEARS at the National Theatre, HAMLET at the Nuffield Theatre, THE DWARFS at the Tricycle, ROMEO AND JULIET on tour, SWEAT at the Bloomsbury and AS YOU LIKE IT in Oxford.

CAOLAN BYRNE / MR THOMAS SCANLON MP

THEATRE includes: THE TEMPEST and LOVE'S LABOURS LOST (Guildford Shakespeare Company), THE PLAYBOY OF THE WESTERN WORLD (Nuffield Southampton), THE FLAGS (Hull Truck), A TALE FOR WINTER (Quicksilver), KING LEAR, ROMEO AND JULIET, and MACBETH at the RSC.

TV/FILM includes: THE COMEDIAN, ROUND IRELAND WITH A FRIDGE, MR NICE and THE MESSAGE.

RUFUS WRIGHT / MR WD Harbinson

TELEVISION includes: EASTENDERS, NEW TRICKS, MIRANDA, WHITE VAN MAN, FIVE DAUGHTERS, THE THICK OF IT, TAKING THE FLAK, EXTRAS, THE BILL, FANNY HILL, DOCTORS, and QUATERMASS EXPERIMENT.

FILM includes: SWINGING WITH THE FINKELS, THE SPECIAL RELATIONSHIP, JEAN CHARLES, QUANTUM OF SOLACE, and SPY GAME.

THEATRE includes: THE 39 STEPS at the Criterion Theatre, THE EMPIRE at the Royal Court, and SERIOUS MONEY at the Birmingham Rep, PRIVATE LIVES at Hampstead, FROST/NIXON and MARY STUART at the Donmar and West End, JOURNEY'S END, West End, HAY FEVER at Basingstoke Haymarket.

TIMOTHY CHIPPING / Reginald Lee

TELEVISION includes: EASTENDERS, THORNE, LAW AND ORDER, TEN DAYS TO WAR, JONATHAN CREEK, AMERICAN EMBASSY, MENACE, HOLBY CITY, CASUALTY, and THE BILL.

FILM includes: SHOOT ON SIGHT, TROY, and CAPTAIN JACK.

THEATRE includes: JOURNEY'S END, tour and West End, DESIRE UNDER THE ELMS at the New Vic Stoke, THE CRUCIBLE, TWELFTH NIGHT, THE COMEDY OF ERRORS all at the RSC, ORESTES for Shared Experience, LEAR at Sheffield Crucible, TAMBURLAINE at Bristol Old Vic, WOYZECK, THE ROBBERS at the Gate Theatre, ROMEO AND JULIET at Liverpool Playhouse, and CAVALCADE and STALINLAND at Citizen's Theatre Glasgow.

KEVIN TRAINOR / Charles Joughin

FILM includes: HELLBOY, THE HOLE and PIES DAY.

TELEVISION includes: THE CAFÉ (Series 1 and 2), SHERLOCK: HOUNDS OF THE BASKERVILLES, JOHN ADAMS (Golden Globe: Best Mini Series), TRIPPING OVER, THE CATHERINE TATE SHOW, THE COMMANDER: BLACK DOG, TITANIC: BIRTH OF A LEGEND.

THEATRE includes: THE PLAYBOY OF THE WESTERN WORLD at the Old Vic. BY JEEVES at the Landor Theatre, CANARY at Liverpool Everyman and Hampstead, LOST MONSTERS at Liverpool Everyman, SIX DEGREES OF SEPARATION at the Old Vic, BENT in the West End, and GLADIATOR GAMES at Stratford East, TWELFTH NIGHT, SOLSTICE, THE COMEDY OF ERRORS, ERIC LA RUE all at the RSC.

JACK BEALE / John Hart

THEATRE includes: TROILUS AND CRESSIDA at the RSC, WINTER at Soho Theatre, 25 DOWN at the Royal Court, TOM'S MIDNIGHT GARDEN at Nottingham Playhouse, BRIEF ENCOUNTER for Kneehigh Theatre, THE WIND IN THE WILLOWS and SPEND SPEND SPEND (UK Tour) at the Watermill Theatre, GRIMM TALES at the Library Theatre Manchester, ALICE at Sheffield Crucible, and TWELFTH NIGHT for Ludlow Festival.

FILM includes: I OF THE LOST.

TV includes: DOCTORS.

THOMAS HOWES / George Symons

THEATRE includes: THE WINSLOW BOY at Theatre Royal Bath, ALADDIN for Ohyesitis Productions, THE HISTORY BOYS (National Theatre/UK Tour), MY FAVOURITE YEAR, BLACK COMEDY, INHERIT THE WIND, A CHORUS OF DISAPPROVAL, MACBETH, TALES FROM OVID, MAN OF LA MANCHA, THE LAST DAYS OF DON JUAN, THE GAME OF LOVE AND CHANCE, THE ISLAND OF SLAVE, THE BACCHAI, THE JUGULAR PROJECT, CLOUD 9, THREE SISTERS all at Guildhall.

TELEVISION includes: UNITED, DOWNTON ABBEY (Series 1 & 2), RED RIDING 1983, and ARMISTICE 90.

FILM includes: UNITED.

JAY VILLIERS / Sir Cosmo Duff Gordon

THEATRE includes: FANTA ORANGE at Finborough Theatre, IN PRAISE OF LOVE at Northampton Theatre Royal, A MIDSUMMER NIGHT'S DREAM, HAMLET, MUCH ADO ABOUT NOTHING all at The Tobacco Factory Bristol, GONE TO EARTH for Shared Experience Tour/Lyric Hammersmith, BARBARIANS and BETRAYAL at Bristol Old Vic, THE TAMING OF THE SHREW at Salisbury Playhouse, HELPING HARRY at Jermyn Street Theatre, HAMLET, MUCH ADO ABOUT NOTHING and AS YOU LIKE IT for Kenneth Branagh's Renaissance Theatre Company.

TELEVISION includes: LEWIS, HEARTBEAT, BONEKICKERS, MIDSOMER MURDERS, THE BILL, THE SECRET PYRAMID OF TUCUME, SILENT WITNESS, EXTRAS, THE MANEATING LEOPARD OF RUDRAPRAYING, THE GOVERNMENT INSPECTOR, ABSOLUTE POWER and THE BRONTES.

FILM includes: THE BEST EXOTIC MARIGOLD HOTEL, THE DIVIDED HEART, THE INTERNATIONAL,

VIRGIN TERRITORY, BEFORE THE RAIN, HENRY V.

ANDREA IRVINE / Lady Duff Gordon

FILM/TELEVISION includes: SIX DEGREES, AT WATER'S EDGE, LOVE HATE II, TWO HEARTS and STELLA DAY.

THEATRE includes: THE REAL THING, HEDDA GABLER, ANNA KARENINA all at the Gate Theatre Dublin, CURSE OF THE STARVING CLASS, PERVE, THE EAST PIER, MACBETH (Irish Times Theatre Award Nomination for Best Supporting Actress), all for the Abbey Theatre Dublin. LIFE IS A DREAM, BONEFIRE, THE WHISPERERS, PENTECOST, THE WAY OF THE WORLD, THE TEMPEST all for Rough Magic Theatre Company.

JAMES TUCKER / Charles Lightoller

TELEVISION includes: AGATHA CHRISTIE, SILENT WITNESS.

THEATRE includes: AMERICAN TRADE, ANTHONY AND CLEOPATRA, AS YOU LIKE IT, KING LEAR, THE GRAIN STORE, EASTWOOD HO!, THE MALCONTENT, EDWARD III, ISLAND PRINCESS, HENRY IV PARTS I, II, III, THE LION, THE WITCH AND THE WARDROBE all for the RSC, IVANOV at the Donmar and Wyndhams, A MIS-SUMMER NIGHT'S DREAM at Sheffield Crucible, HINGE OF THE WORLD at Yvonne Arnaud Theatre .

PATRICK O' KANE / Joseph Ismay

FILM includes: PROMETHEUS, PERKINS 14, EXORCIST-THE BEGINNINGS, CHARLOTTE'S RED, STEALING REMBRANDT, OCTANE, THOUGH THE SKY FALLS, WONDERFUL WORLD and SUNSET HEIGHTS.

TELEVISION includes: GAME OF THRONES, THE BORGIAS, HOLBY BLUE, WIRE IN THE BLOOD, FIVE DAYS, WAKING THE DEAD, HOLBY CITY, GUNPOWDER-TREASON AND PLOT and THE WAYFARER.

THEATRE includes: 16 POSSIBLE GLIMPSEs at the Peacock Theatre, THE CRUCIBLE at the Lyric Theatre, DR FAUSTUS at the Royal Exchange Theatre, WAR HORSE at the National Theatre and West End, Macbeth for the RSC, COLD COMFORT at the Lyric Belfast and London, WHISTLE IN THE DARK at the Royal Exchange and Tricycle Theatre, HAMLET at the Abbey and Lyric.

JAMES HILLIER / Sir Ernest Shackleton

THEATRE includes: IN THE LAND OF UZ/66 BOOKS at the Bush Theatre. BLUE SURGE at the Finborough (nominated for an Off West End (OFFIE) Award), CLOSER at Northampton Royal Theatre, THE HOMECOMING at Royal Exchange and LULU at the Almeida Theatre.

FILM includes: THE KING'S HEAD, FIRED, LOCOCK, SIMON'S MAKING A FILM and FATHERS OF GIRLS, STAGKNIGHT, TOMORROW'S FORECAST, SEX AND LIES, FOUR FEATHERS, LONG TIME DEAD and RUNNING TIME.

TELEVISION includes: CITY ON FIRE, CASUALTY, SURVIVORS, EASTENDERS, HOLBY BLUE SERIES 2, HOLBY BLUE SERIES 1, GOLDPLATED, THE BILL, THE RISE AND FALL OF ROME: REVOLUTION, BLACKBEARD, SERIOUS AND ORGANISED and THE INSPECTOR LYNLEY MYSTERIES.

Chief Executive

Anne McReynolds

Creative Programmes

Gillian Mitchell	Director of Programmes
Hugh Mulholland	Curatorial Consultant
Stuart Campbell	Programming Officer
Clare Lawlor	Learning and Participation Officer
Samantha Porciello	Learning and Participation Officer
Eoin Dara	Curatorial Assistant
Simon Bird	Technical Manager
Damian Hughes	Assistant Technical Manager
Christopher McCorry	Technician

Marketing & Communications

Áine McVerry	Director of Marketing and Communications
Maeve Lewis	Marketing Manager
Christine Bowen	Media and Communications Officer
Martin Forker	Business Development Manager
Billy Partridge	Box Office Manager
Angela Mahon	Box Office Assistant
Stuart Roberts	Box Office Assistant

Finance & Operations

Caroline Rooney	Director of Finance and Operations
Fran Cavanagh	Operations Manager
Nigel McCartney	House Manager
Andrea Mullin	Admin and HR Officer
Jason Horsfield	Finance Officer

Owen McCafferty
Titanic

Scenes from the
British Wreck Commissioner's Inquiry
1912

faber and faber

First published in 2012
by Faber and Faber Limited
74–77 Great Russell Street
London WC1B 3DA

Typeset by Country Setting, Kingsdown, Kent CT14 8ES
Printed and bound by CPI Group (UK) Ltd, Croydon, CR0 4YY

A CIP record for this book
is available from the British Library

ISBN 978–0–571–29508–1

FSC
www.fsc.org
MIX
Paper from
responsible sources
FSC® C101712

2 4 6 8 10 9 7 5 3 1

Author's Note

I approached this project not as an historian or a journalist but as a playwright. This is not an historical document, it is a play. While I have at all times tried not to interfere with the content of what a character is saying, I have on occasion, for the sake of clarity, changed how they might say it. I have also used the same style of punctuation I always use when writing any play. And for practical and artistic purposes I added a fictional character. As is the nature of these plays I have left out far more than I included.

Characters

Sir Cosmo Duff Gordon
forty-nine, first-class passenger, only one eye

Lady Duff Gordon
forty-eight, first-class passenger

Charles Lightoller
thirty-eight, born Lancashire, Second Officer

Joseph Ismay
forty-nine, born Liverpool, first-class passenger,
Managing Director of Oceanic Steam Navigation Co.

Sir Ernest Shackleton
thirty-eight, born Co. Kildare, explorer

Clerk of the Court
(fictional character)

Place
Scottish Hall, Buckingham Gate, Westminster

Time
May–July 1912

The Clerk of the Court is dressed in a present-day suit
and does not wear a tie.

When a character withdraws they should remain on stage
and go to what might be a viewing gallery.

*This text went to press before the end of rehearsals,
so may differ slightly from the play as performed.*

TITANIC

Act One

Clerk eight hundred bundles of fresh asparagus – a
parisian cafe – forty tons of potatoes – seven thousand
five hundred blankets – a heated swimming pool – one
thousand two hundred teapots – twenty thousand bottles
of beer and stout – five grand pianos – a turkish bath –
one hundred pairs of grape scissors – forty-five thousand
table napkins – one thousand five hundred bottles of
wine – a gymnasium – forty thousand fresh eggs – two
barber's shops with automatic hair-drying appliances –
seventy-five thousand pounds of fresh meat – one
thousand oyster forks – nine hundred tons of baggage
and freight – more than three million rivets – and four
cases of opium – i am a fictional character by the way –
of the now – the present – i do not sit in judgement –
functional not emotional – a made-up clerk of the court –
the rest is real – or as real as can be made – or wanted –
1912 – no more than a few weeks after the titanic sank
on her maiden voyage across the north atlantic to new
york – two inquiries – one in new york and one in london
– we are in london – the counsel – the questioners – the
truth-seekers etc

The five men enter and stand at their chairs.

the man in charge – the commissioner – lord mersey (*Sits.*)
– the attorney general – sir rufus isaacs (*Sits.*) – the solicitor
general – sir j simon (*Sits.*) – mr thomas scanlon mp –
acting on behalf of the national sailors' and firemen's
union of great britain and ireland (*Sits.*) – and mr w d
harbinson acting on behalf of third-class passengers –
there are of course others but we had no room for them

9

Reginald Lee enters.

Clerk day 4 – reginald lee – lookout on the titanic – the attorney general

The Attorney General stands.

Attorney General are you an able seaman

Reginald Lee yes

Attorney General and were you on the titanic when she sailed in april on her first voyage

Reginald Lee yes

Attorney General you were the lookout man

Reginald Lee yes

Attorney General you have had about fifteen or sixteen years at sea altogether

Reginald Lee yes

Attorney General have you acted as lookout man in other ships before the titanic

Reginald Lee yes

Attorney General have you ever had glasses for use as lookout man

Reginald Lee yes – but i do not know whether they were private or supplied by the company

Attorney General have you found them of use

Reginald Lee they are better than the ordinary eyesight

Attorney General do you know if they are supplied in any other vessels of the white star line

Reginald Lee i cannot say for certain – but my mate in the crow's nest who was for four years in the oceanic as lookout man – told me they had them there

Attorney General were there any on the titanic

Reginald Lee no – not for our use anyway

Attorney General was there any place in the crow's nest for glasses

Reginald Lee yes

Attorney General on the titanic

Reginald Lee yes there was a small box

Attorney General if i understand you right – there was a box there for glasses but no glasses in the box

Reginald Lee i could not tell you if they were for glasses – but there was a box there that would hold glasses

Attorney General did you look for glasses at all in the crow's nest

Reginald Lee we asked for them

Attorney General on the titanic

Reginald Lee yes – i did not personally ask for them but one of the other fellows did – and they said there were none for us

Attorney General who was one of the other fellows who asked for them – do you know

Reginald Lee symons or jewell – i cannot be sure which one it was

Attorney General i think we know symons was jewell's mate on the lookout

Reginald Lee yes

Attorney General fleet was yours

Reginald Lee yes

Attorney General and i think hogg and evans were the other two

Reginald Lee yes

Attorney General did you come on the lookout at ten o'clock

Reginald Lee yes

Attorney General on sunday night the 14th april

Reginald Lee yes

Attorney General how long did you remain on the lookout – what was your duty

Reginald Lee four to six and ten to twelve

Attorney General i suppose that would mean that you and fleet came on at ten o'clock

Reginald Lee yes

Attorney General and relieved symons and jewell?

Reginald Lee yes

Attorney General did one of you take the starboard side and one the port side of the crow's nest on the lookout

Reginald Lee i generally took the starboard side and fleet took the port side

Attorney General you were on the starboard side – do you know whether there was any other lookout than you two

Reginald Lee i could not say – we do not know what orders are given from the bridge

Attorney General then when you relieved jewell and symons did they pass any word to you

Reginald Lee yes – they told us to keep a careful lookout for ice and growlers in particular

Attorney General they told you to keep a careful look out for ice and growlers

Reginald Lee yes – by the officer of the watch before ten o'clock - mr lightoller

Attorney General what sort of night was it

Reginald Lee a clear starry night overhead – but at the time of the accident there was a haze right ahead

Attorney General at the time of the accident a haze right ahead

Reginald Lee a haze right ahead – in fact it was extending more or less round the horizon – there was no moon

Attorney General and no wind

Reginald Lee and no wind whatever – barring what the ship made herself

Attorney General quite a calm sea

Reginald Lee quite a calm sea

Attorney General was it cold

Reginald Lee very – freezing

Attorney General colder than you had had it yet on the voyage

Reginald Lee i would not say that – but it was the coldest we had had that voyage – yes

Attorney General it was the coldest that night than ever you had had it that voyage in the titanic

Reginald Lee yes – on that trip

Attorney General did you notice this haze which you said extended on the horizon when you first came on the lookout – or did it come later

Reginald Lee it was not so distinct then not to be noticed – you did not really notice it then – not on going on watch – but we had all our work cut out to pierce through it just after we started – my mate happened to pass the remark to me – he said – well if we can see through that we'll be lucky – that was when we began to notice there was a haze on the water – there was nothing in sight

Attorney General you had been told of course to keep a careful lookout for ice – and you were trying to pierce the haze as much as you could

Reginald Lee yes – to see as much as we could

Attorney General at the time you came on watch – up to the moment just before the collision – can you tell us whether there was any difference in the speed at which the vessel was travelling compared with the rest of the voyage – what i mean is was she going the same speed

Reginald Lee she seemed to be going at the same rate all the way

Attorney General before half past eleven on that watch – that is seven bells – had you reported anything at all – do you remember

Reginald Lee there was nothing to be reported

Attorney General then what was the first thing you did report

Reginald Lee the first thing that was reported was after seven bells struck – it was some minutes – it might have been nine or ten minutes afterwards – three bells were struck by fleet warning – right ahead – and immediately he rung the telephone up to the bridge – iceberg right ahead – the reply came back from the bridge – thank you

Commissioner that would be about eleven forty

Attorney General that is right my lord – ten minutes after seven bells – (*To Witness.*) i want you to tell the story from this point – you were watching the iceberg

Reginald Lee yes

Attorney General did you notice what the ship did

Reginald Lee as soon as the reply came back – thank you the helm must have been put hard-a-starboard or very close to it – because she veered to the port – and it seemed almost as if she might clear it – but i suppose there was ice under water

Commissioner she veered to port – her helm must have been put hard-a-starboard

Reginald Lee yes

Attorney General you saw the iceberg as the vessel veered to port did you

Reginald Lee i saw it before that

Attorney General where did you get the iceberg – on what side of you

Reginald Lee on the starboard hand as she was veering to port

Attorney General you had the iceberg on the starboard side

Reginald Lee yes

Attorney General you were on the starboard side of the crow's nest you told us

Reginald Lee just at that time i happened to be right in front of the nest – because as the nest is semicircular the telephone is in the corner of the nest on the starboard side – my mate was telephoning from there – and i was standing in front of the nest watching the berg

Attorney General do you mean you were standing just about amidships

Reginald Lee just about amidships in front of the nest

Attorney General you were watching the berg – you had got the berg on the starboard side as the vessel's head was veered to port

Reginald Lee yes

Attorney General and you watched it

Reginald Lee i watched it

Attorney General now could you give us any idea of what height there was of ice out of the water – i only want to have some idea of it

Reginald Lee it was higher than the forecastle – but i could not say what height was clear of the water

Commissioner how far does the forecastle stand out of the water

Attorney General i think it is about sixty feet

Commissioner i do not think it is as much as sixty feet

Attorney General i think she drew about thirty-four feet

Commissioner i was not thinking about her draught but how high the forecastle would stand from the water

Attorney General i said sixty feet i am told it is about fifty-five feet (*To Witness.*) can you give us any idea of the breadth – what did it look like – it was something which was above the forecastle

Reginald Lee it was a dark mass that came through the haze and there was no white appearing until it was just close alongside the ship – and that was just a fringe at the top

Attorney General can you give us an idea – to the best of your ability – how far off she was when you passed her to starboard

Reginald Lee she hit us

Attorney General how far was the vessel from the iceberg

Reginald Lee what did you say

Attorney General you have told us your vessel veered to port and then you got the iceberg on the starboard side

Reginald Lee yes – that is where she hit

Attorney General quite so – that is where she hit – but can you tell us how far the iceberg was from you – this mass that you saw

Reginald Lee it might have been half a mile or more – it might have been less – i could not give you the distance in that peculiar light

Attorney General you are speaking of when it was you first saw it

Reginald Lee yes

Attorney General i understand that – you think it might have been half a mile or less – and of course you cannot give any better indication than that – i am much obliged to you for that – but it is not quite what i wanted you to tell us – you have told us that she veered to port and then she struck on the starboard side – but when you were looking at her could you see whether this darkness which you have told us of was any distance from the ship or was it quite close up against the side of the ship

Reginald Lee close up against the side of the ship on the starboard bow

Attorney General give us – to the best of your ability –

where it was according to you the vessel struck – i want to get some idea from you

Reginald Lee just before the foremast – it must have been there because when i went down from the crow's nest – the water was coming into – i do not know whether you call it number one or number two – it was level with here (*Pointing to model.*) that is about where it was

The Attorney General sits.

Mr Scanlon stands.

Mr Scanlon when you are at sea in a fog is it a usual practice to station a watchman at the bows in addition to the lookout in the crow's nest

Reginald Lee the captain of the ship has to be responsible for that kind of thing

Mr Scanlon just tell me whether in your experience it is usual to do that

Reginald Lee if the captain of the ship thinks it is necessary

Mr Scanlon have you seen it done

Reginald Lee i have

Mr Scanlon have you seen it done frequently

Reginald Lee not frequently

Mr Scanlon is not a haze a kind of fog

Reginald Lee it is a kind of fog but you could not describe it as a fog

Commissioner (*to Witness*) were you in a fog when this accident happened

Reginald Lee no

Mr Scanlon did you communicate with the bridge that you found it hazy

Reginald Lee no

Mr Scanlon were you not then of the opinion that the pressure of that haze made the passage dangerous

Reginald Lee i am not the officer of the watch

Mr Scanlon did you not think it a proper thing to communicate with the officer on the bridge

Reginald Lee certainly not – the officer of the watch would ask you what you meant by it – he would ask you whether you were interfering with his duty or not

Mr Scanlon when you are going through a haze at night is it usual to slow up – slacken speed

Reginald Lee that has nothing to do with me – i am not on the bridge – i am a lookout man – as i said before

Mr Scanlon you have often been in fog i daresay in atlantic passages

Reginald Lee i am in a fog now

Mr Scanlon would it have been easier to have observed the iceberg from the bow than from the crow's nest

Reginald Lee i cannot answer you that

Mr Scanlon when you have been on other ships have you ever been at watch on the bows

Reginald Lee yes

Commissioner was there a crow's nest on that ship

Reginald Lee yes

Commissioner and was there somebody in the crow's nest as well

Reginald Lee yes

Commissioner and somebody on the bridge as well

Reginald Lee that was off the banks of newfoundland

Commissioner was there somebody on the bridge as well

Reginald Lee two quartermasters were there and the officer of the watch

Mr Scanlon as you have been stationed both in the crow's nest and in other ships on the bows i want you to give us your opinion as to whether it would be easier to see the iceberg if you were stationed at the bows than in the crow's nest

Commissioner he has given you an answer to that which i believe to be quite true – that he does not

Mr Scanlon sits.

Mr Harbinson stands.

Mr Harbinson i believe you went from southampton to cherbourg

Reginald Lee yes

Mr Harbinson did you take many passengers on at cherbourg

Reginald Lee that i could not say

Mr Harbinson you do not know

Reginald Lee no

Mr Harbinson then you went from cherbourg to queenstown

Reginald Lee yes

Mr Harbinson did you ship many passengers at queenstown

Reginald Lee a good number but i cannot say how many

Mr Harbinson but a good number

Reginald Lee yes

Mr Harbinson mainly i suppose third-class passengers

Reginald Lee yes third-class passengers

Mr Harbinson do i rightly understand that third-class passengers were carried both fore and aft in the titanic

Commissioner you do – you need not wait for an answer to that

Mr Harbinson thank you your lordship (*To Witness.*)

you were told to look out for ice and growlers

Reginald Lee quite so

Mr Harbinson had you been told there was ice about

Reginald Lee yes

Mr Harbinson you knew that ice was about

Reginald Lee you could smell it

Commissioner smell it

Mr Harbinson that is his reply

Commissioner this is the first time i have heard that – does he mean that he felt the cold – (*To Witness.*) is that what you mean by smell

Reginald Lee there was a sudden change in temperature my lord

Commissioner then i understand

Mr Harbinson despite the fact that this haze was about you saw no slackening in speed

Reginald Lee no

Mr Harbinson and no alteration of the course

Reginald Lee no

Mr Harbinson immediately after the collision did you come down from the crow's nest

Reginald Lee no i waited until our relief came up at twelve o'clock

Commissioner you are taking him all over the same story again – he came down from the crow's nest at twelve o'clock – the end of his watch

Mr Harbinson immediately you came down from the crow's nest did you see any passengers come from the fore part of the boat

Reginald Lee no because underneath the forecastle you would not see anybody there – only the sailor folk or some of the firemen

Mr Harbinson did you see anybody giving any instructions or warnings to the passengers in that part of the boat

Reginald Lee i saw the bosun and he sent the watch up on deck to clear the boats

Mr Harbinson but you did not hear any instructions given as to warnings to be given to the passengers

Reginald Lee no

  Mr Harbinson sits.

Commissioner is your eyesight good

Reginald Lee i think so my lord

Commissioner do you believe that it is good

Reginald Lee i do

Commissioner can you tell me the difference between day binoculars and night binoculars

Reginald Lee no my lord – except that they are made in the trade for night use and day use

Clerk the witness withdraws

Charles Joughin enters.

Clerk day six – charles joughin – chief baker on the titanic – the solicitor general

The Solicitor General stands.

Solicitor General were you the chief baker on the titanic

Charles Joughin yes

Solicitor General what was the staff of bakers under you

Charles Joughin thirteen

Solicitor General thirteen and yourself as chief baker

Charles Joughin yes

Solicitor General i suppose if provision were wanted it would be your department to look after that would it not

Charles Joughin no

Solicitor General what about bread

Charles Joughin the boats are provided with hard bread – what we call biscuits

Solicitor General did not you hear any orders given about provisions for the boats

Charles Joughin not directly from any officer – word was passed down from the top deck and i received it eventually through other channels

Solicitor General what was it

Charles Joughin provision boats – or put any spare provisions you have in the boats – that was it

Solicitor General as i understand – the biscuits – the hard bread – would be in the boats already – or ought to be

Charles Joughin yes

Solicitor General and it would only be the soft bread you had to think about

Charles Joughin any surplus stuff we had around that was handy we would put into the boats

Solicitor General you heard that order passed along – did you take steps to send up some provisions to the boats

Charles Joughin yes

Solicitor General what was it you did – you and your men

Charles Joughin i sent thirteen men up with four loaves apiece – forty pounds of bread each as near as i could guess

Solicitor General and your staff – your men – had they got stations for the boats

Charles Joughin yes

Solicitor General and as far as you know did they know their stations

Charles Joughin yes

Solicitor General did these thirteen bakers go up with these loaves

Charles Joughin yes

Solicitor General did you go up to the deck yourself

Charles Joughin i stayed in the shop for a little while and then i followed them up the middle staircase

Solicitor General just two or three questions about what happened after that – which was your boat

Charles Joughin i was assigned to number ten

Solicitor General did you go to your boat – number ten

Charles Joughin yes

Solicitor General were there passengers there

Charles Joughin a good many passengers there

Solicitor General was the order good – the discipline good

Charles Joughin splendid

Solicitor General number ten was being got ready – when you saw it had anybody got into the boat yet

Charles Joughin no

Solicitor General now tell us about number ten in order – what happened

Charles Joughin it was swung out – the stewards firemen and sailors all got in a line – we passed the ladies through

Solicitor General into number ten

Charles Joughin into number ten – then we got it about half full and then we had difficulty in finding ladies for it – they ran away from the boat and said they were safer where they were

Solicitor General you heard ladies saying that

Charles Joughin i am sure of that

Commissioner when the boat was half full we had difficulty in finding more ladies

Charles Joughin right sir

Commissioner they ran away saying they were safer where they were

Charles Joughin yes

Solicitor General up to this time could you tell me had you seen any third-class passengers – women from the third class

Charles Joughin yes sir – plenty

Solicitor General so far as you saw was any distinction made between the classes – first-class ladies or second-class ladies or third-class ladies

Charles Joughin none at all

Solicitor General of course at ordinary times this boat deck is a first-class deck – a promenade – is it not

Charles Joughin yes

Solicitor General and the third-class people would not get on to it

Charles Joughin it is railed off just from the boats – and the saloon passengers use it as a sunning deck

Solicitor General but at this time were there any barriers up

Charles Joughin no

Solicitor General you know the way – i suppose – that third-class passengers would have to go in order to get on to this top deck – they would have to mount stairs would not they

Charles Joughin they have to go up some stairs – but there is an emergency door from the third class into the second class leading up the broad staircase that was open very early

Solicitor General just tell us please how is it you know that emergency door was open for them

Charles Joughin because i went down that way to my room after shutting the bakery door

Solicitor General when you went down to your room and found this door open did you at that time see third-class people coming up

Charles Joughin coming along the alleyway – some women – with two bags in their hands – they would not let go of them

Solicitor General now just let us go back to boat number ten and finish it – you said that when it was about half full with women you could not find more women to pass along the line and put into the boat

Charles Joughin we had difficulty in finding them

Solicitor General what was done – what happened

Charles Joughin i myself and three or four other chaps went on the next deck and forcibly brought up women and children

Solicitor General did not they want to go

Charles Joughin no sir – they were all sitting squatting down on the deck

Solicitor General did you put them into the boat

Charles Joughin we threw them in – the boat was standing off about a yard and a half from the ship's side – with a slight list – we could not put them in – we could either hand them in or just drop them in

Solicitor General did that fill your boat or was there still room

Charles Joughin eventually it was filled – pretty well filled anyway

Solicitor General you did not i think go away in that boat

Charles Joughin no

Solicitor General although it was your boat

Charles Joughin i was supposed to be captain of the boat by the crew list

Solicitor General why was it that you did not get in

Charles Joughin well i was standing waiting for orders from the officer to jump in and then he ordered two sailors in and a steward – a steward named burke – i was waiting for orders to get into the boat – but they evidently thought it was full enough and i did not get in

Solicitor General and then where did you go

Charles Joughin i went – scouting around – as we call it

Solicitor General and then you went below

Charles Joughin yes

Solicitor General now we just want to finish your experience – you say you went below after number ten had gone – did you stay below or did you come up again

Charles Joughin i went down to my room and had a drop of liqueur that i had down there – and while i was there i saw the old doctor and spoke to him and then i came upstairs again

Solicitor General on to the boat deck

Charles Joughin yes on to the boat deck

Solicitor General just tell us shortly what you did

Charles Joughin i saw that all the boats had gone – i saw that all the boats were away

Solicitor General that all the boats had gone

Charles Joughin yes that all the boats had gone

Solicitor General do you mean forward as well as aft

Charles Joughin i could not see very well forward and i did not look – because they went off first as far as i could understand

Solicitor General at all events all the boats had gone

Charles Joughin yes

Solicitor General yes – what next

Charles Joughin i went down on to b deck – the deckchairs were lying all along and i started throwing deckchairs through the large ports

Solicitor General what did you do with the deckchairs

Charles Joughin i threw them through the large ports

Solicitor General threw them overboard

Charles Joughin yes

Solicitor General they would float i suppose

Charles Joughin yes

Solicitor General i think one sees why – just to make it clear why did you do that

Charles Joughin it was an idea of my own

Solicitor General tell us why – was it to give something to cling to

Charles Joughin i was looking out for something for myself sir

Solicitor General quite so – did you throw a whole lot of them overboard

Charles Joughin i should say about fifty

Solicitor General were other people helping you to do it

Charles Joughin i did not see them

Solicitor General you were alone – as far as you could see

Charles Joughin there was other people on the deck – but i did not see anybody else throwing chairs over

Solicitor General then after having thrown these deckchairs overboard did you go up to the boat again

Charles Joughin i went to the deck pantry

Solicitor General tell us what happened

Charles Joughin i went to the deck pantry and while i was in there i thought i would take a drink of water – and while i was getting the drink of water i heard a kind of a crush – as if something had buckled – as if part of the ship had buckled – and then i heard a rush overhead

Solicitor General do you mean a rush of people

Charles Joughin yes – a rush of people overhead on the deck

Solicitor General you could hear it

Charles Joughin yes

Solicitor General people running – yes

Charles Joughin when i got up on top i could see them clambering down from those decks – of course i was in the tail end of the rush

Commissioner clambering down – climbing down from where

Charles Joughin (*shows on model*) these rails and steps – they came down this way

Solicitor General they had run along as far aft as they could on the boat deck

Charles Joughin yes

Solicitor General did you see them clambering down to get on to the a deck so as to get further aft

Charles Joughin their idea was to get on to the poop

Solicitor General you say that you heard this sound of buckling or crackling – was it loud – could anybody in the ship hear it

Charles Joughin you could have heard it but you did not really know what it was – it was not an explosion or anything like that – it was like as if the iron was parting

Solicitor General like the breaking of metal

Charles Joughin yes

Solicitor General was it immediately after that sound that you heard this rushing of people and saw them climbing up

Charles Joughin yes

Solicitor General what did you do

Charles Joughin i kept out of the crush as much as i possibly could and i followed down – followed down – getting towards the well of the deck – and just as i got down towards the well she gave a great list over to port and threw everybody in a bunch – except myself – i did not see anybody else besides myself out of the bunch

Solicitor General it is very difficult to say how many i daresay – but – could you give me some idea of how many people there were in this crush

Charles Joughin i have no idea sir – i know they were piled up

Solicitor General what do you mean when you say no idea – were there hundreds

Charles Joughin yes – there were more than that – many hundreds i should say

Solicitor General can you tell us what happened to you

Charles Joughin yes i eventually got on to the starboard side of the poop

Commissioner will you point out to me where you got to

Charles Joughin (*showing on model*) this is where i eventually got to

Solicitor General did you find anybody else holding that rail there – on the poop

Charles Joughin no

Solicitor General you were the only one

Charles Joughin i did not see anybody else

Solicitor General were you holding the rail so that you were inside the ship – or were you holding the rail so that you were on the outside of the ship

Charles Joughin on the outside

Solicitor General then what happened

Charles Joughin well i was just wondering what next to do – i had tightened my belt and i had transferred some things out of this pocket into my stern pocket – i was just wondering what next to do when she went

Solicitor General and did you find yourself in the water

Charles Joughin yes

Solicitor General did you feel that you were dragged under or did you keep on top of the water

Charles Joughin i do not believe my head went under the water at all – it may have been wetted but no more

Solicitor General are you a good swimmer

Charles Joughin yes

Solicitor General how long do you think you were in the water before you got anything to hold on to

Charles Joughin i did not attempt to get anything to hold on to until i reached a collapsible – but that was daylight

Solicitor General daylight – was it

Charles Joughin i do not know what time it was

Solicitor General then you were in the water for a long long time

Charles Joughin i should say over two hours sir

Solicitor General were you trying to make progress in the water – to swim – or just keeping where you were

Charles Joughin i was just paddling and treading water

Solicitor General and then daylight broke

Charles Joughin yes

Solicitor General did you see any icebergs about you

Charles Joughin no sir – i could not see anything

Solicitor General did it keep calm till daylight or did the wind rise at all

Charles Joughin it was just like a pond

Solicitor General then you spoke of a collapsible boat – tell us shortly about it

Charles Joughin just as it was breaking daylight i saw what i thought was some wreckage and i started to swim towards it slowly – when i got near enough i found it was a collapsible – not properly upturned but on its side – with an officer and i should say about twenty or twenty-five men standing on top of it

Commissioner with an officer and what

Charles Joughin i should say roughly about twenty-five men standing on the top – well on the side not on the top

Solicitor General do you know which officer it was

Charles Joughin yes – mr lightoller

Solicitor General mr lightoller and you think about twenty or twenty-five people

Charles Joughin yes

Commissioner men – he said

Solicitor General yes men my lord

Charles Joughin yes all men

Solicitor General you said something about its being turned on its side

Charles Joughin yes

Solicitor General i wish you would explain what you mean

Charles Joughin (*pointing to model*) it was like as if one of those lifeboats was on its side – floating on its side

Solicitor General then they were not in the boat were they

Charles Joughin no

Solicitor General they were . . .

Charles Joughin standing on the side – holding one another's shoulders

Solicitor General did you swim towards it

Charles Joughin yes

Solicitor General was there any room for you

Charles Joughin no sir

Solicitor General you agree do you that there really was no room for you

Charles Joughin there was not room

Solicitor General and so they could not take you in

Charles Joughin there was no room for any more – they were standing on it then

Solicitor General do you stay near

Charles Joughin i tried to get on it but i was pushed off it – and i what you call hung around it

Solicitor General how much later on was it that you were picked up

Charles Joughin i eventually got round to the opposite side and a cook that was on the collapsible recognised me – and he held out his hand and held me – a chap named maynard

Solicitor General was he able to pull you out of the water – or was he only just able to help to support you

Charles Joughin no

Solicitor General he gave you a hand and you kept treading water

Charles Joughin no – my lifebelt helped me – and i held on the side of the boat

Solicitor General you had been wearing a lifebelt

Charles Joughin yes all the time

Solicitor General so that your feet would be in the water

Charles Joughin yes – and my legs

Solicitor General and you supported yourself by your lifebelt – i do not want to be harrowing about it – but was the water very cold

Charles Joughin i felt colder in the lifeboat – after i got in the lifeboat

Solicitor General you were picked up were you by a lifeboat later on

Charles Joughin we were hanging on to this collapsible and eventually a lifeboat came in sight

Solicitor General and they took you aboard

Charles Joughin they got within fifty yards and they sung out that they could only take ten – so i said to this maynard let go of my hand and i swam to meet it – so that i would be one of the ten

Solicitor General did you swim to it and were you taken in

Charles Joughin yes i was taken in

Solicitor General you said you thought it was about two hours before you saw this collapsible and then you spent some time on the collapsible – how long do you suppose it was after you got to the collapsible that you were taken into the lifeboat

Charles Joughin i should say we were on the collapsible about half an hour

Solicitor General that means for some two and a half hours you were in the water

Charles Joughin practically – yes

Solicitor General this lifeboat that took you aboard did it also take some men off the collapsible

Charles Joughin yes

Solicitor General you do not know who was in command of the boat that picked you up

Charles Joughin mr lightoller left the collapsible and then took charge of the boat till we reached the carpathia

Solicitor General after you and some of the others were taken on board this lifeboat did that lifeboat rescue any other people that you know of

Charles Joughin no sir – it could not have done

Solicitor General it was too full

Charles Joughin it was filled right up

The Solicitor General sits.

Mr Harbinson stands.

Mr Harbinson when the boat gave this lurch that you have described to us you say a great many people were thrown into one bunch – have you any idea of the class of passengers they were

Charles Joughin i could not say

Mr Harbinson sits.

The Solicitor General stands.

Solicitor General there is one other thing – you may be able to tell us about the electric light in the afterpart of the ship – you have described how you heard the breaking of the metal – the rending of metal – followed by this rush of people to the poop – at the time when you heard the rending of metal were the electric lights burning in the part of the ship you saw

Charles Joughin the electric were burning right to the very last – i saw the time by my watch at a quarter past two

Solicitor General you looked at your watch

Charles Joughin yes

Solicitor General you were carrying it

Charles Joughin yes i had it in my pocket – i was transferring it from this pocket to my stern pocket

Solicitor General and you looked at it as you did

Charles Joughin yes

Solicitor General were you holding on to the rail at the time

Charles Joughin no i was getting towards the rail – it was a quarter past two then

Solicitor General and the electric light was burning then

Charles Joughin yes

Solicitor General so that there was never a time when you were on that ship when there was not electric light where you were

Charles Joughin right to the very finish that i saw

The Solicitor General sits.

Clerk the witness withdraws

John Hart enters.

Clerk day nine – john hart – a steward on the titanic – mr harbinson

Mr Harbinson stands.

Mr Harbinson now – i should like to know what are the means employed to prevent the third-class passengers – during the voyage – from straying into the first- and second-class decks and quarters of the ship – first – are there collapsible gates

John Hart yes gates that can be removed – dividing the third-class deck there is a companion – dividing the second-class deck and the first-class deck there is a barrier

Mr Harbinson are those kept fastened during the course of a voyage – the barrier and the companion

John Hart no

Mr Harbinson are they open

John Hart well the barrier that lifts over and the gate that fixes in you can just take it out with your hand – it is never locked

Mr Harbinson do i understand you to say that those gates are not locked at any time and the barrier is not fastened

John Hart not to my knowledge

Mr Harbinson so that at any time a third-class passenger – by pushing the gate or raising the barrier – can go to the second-class deck or to the first-class deck – is that right

John Hart that is correct – that is of course if there is nobody there on watch – there usually is a quartermaster by there – or a seaman

Mr Harbinson have you ever seen those gates locked

John Hart no i was not long enough on the ship to see them locked

Mr Harbinson i mean any other ship – what ship were you on before you came on to this ship

John Hart i have been in the whole four of the american line boats

Mr Harbinson on any of the previous boats have you seen those barriers or gates locked to prevent third-class passengers from straying on to the first- or second-class decks

John Hart you see the ships are all built differently – the american line boats are built entirely differently from the titanic

Mr Harbinson i want to make it quite clear – is it the usual practice on transatlantic passenger steamers to keep the gates locked and the barriers fixed – so that they cannot be opened by third-class passengers

John Hart i do not know of it

Mr Harbinson have you seen it

John Hart i have not seen it

Mr Harbinson how many days had you been on the titanic before the accident took place – what day did you join

John Hart the ship left on the tenth – on the wednesday – i joined the ship on the friday before the wednesday

Mr Harbinson you had been on board a number of days then – and during that time that you had been on board had you looked whether or not those gates were locked or the barriers fixed

John Hart no

Mr Harbinson you had not looked

John Hart no

Mr Harbinson do i rightly understand you to say that you do not know whether they were locked or not – is that the effect of your evidence

John Hart i fail to understand you

Mr Harbinson you did not look whether the gates were locked or the barrier closed from the time you went on the titanic until the time of the accident – is that so

John Hart i do not see how they could be locked – i do not think so at all

Mr Harbinson did you look to see whether the gates were locked or the barriers permanently fixed down

John Hart prior to the accident

Mr Harbinson yes

John Hart no

Mr Harbinson therefore you do not know whether they were or were not

John Hart previous to the accident i cannot answer

Mr Harbinson therefore at the time of the collision you do not know

John Hart no – i say previous to the accident

Mr Harbinson i quite follow you

Commissioner they were all down as i understand when you were bringing the passengers away

John Hart yes my lord

Commissioner all three were opened

John Hart yes my lord

Mr Harbinson did you see anybody open these gates or raise these barriers

John Hart no i did not see anybody open them – but i had to pass through them and i saw them open

Solicitor General not opened – but open

Mr Harbinson you saw them open

John Hart yes

Mr Harbinson you did not see who opened them

John Hart no

Mr Harbinson you saw them open

John Hart yes

Mr Harbinson that was when you were taking up the first batch of third-class passengers

John Hart yes

Mr Harbinson do i gather rightly from you that it was a considerable time after the third-class steward had told you to rouse up your people – that you went about reassuring these people and telling them that the vessel was not hurt

John Hart no – right from the very first we were trying to convince the people that she was not hurt

Mr Harbinson did i understand you rightly when you said that – a large number of men were coming from forward – from the front part of the ship – i went about among my people trying to show them that the vessel was not hurt

John Hart trying to assure not to show them

Mr Harbinson i accept your correction – trying to assure them the vessel was not hurt – is that what you said

John Hart that is so

Mr Harbinson why did you on your own authority –
after you had been told by the first-class steward . . .

John Hart by who

Mr Harbinson by your chief third-class steward to go
down and rouse these people – why did you – upon your
own authority – go round and tell them that the vessel
was not hurt

John Hart it was not on my own authority at all

Mr Harbinson who told you to do that

John Hart the third-class steward told me to get my
people about as quietly as possible

Mr Harbinson why did he tell you to get them up

John Hart i cannot answer why he did – i take it on
account of the collision – he must have had word that
there had been an accident

Mr Harbinson and knowing from him that there must
have been an accident – and that he considered the
accident was of such a character that those people should
be roused – you went around them and tried to assure
them that the vessel was not hurt

John Hart in the first place

Mr Harbinson why did you do that

John Hart because it was my instructions to

Commissioner why

John Hart to keep them quiet – it is quite obvious

Mr Harbinson i put it to you – that it was a result of
these assurances of yours that the people refused to go up
on deck

John Hart you put it to me as such

Mr Harbinson i put it to you that as a result of these assurances given to the people they refused to leave their berths

John Hart i do not take it as such

Mr Harbinson was it so

John Hart it was not so – if you will pay a little attention you will find that some people were taken to the boat deck

Mr Harbinson please do not be impertinent

John Hart i do not wish to be impertinent

Mr Harbinson i suggest to you that it was as a result of these assurances given by you that they were declining to leave their berths

John Hart you take it as such

Mr Harbinson i ask you – is that so

John Hart i do not know

Mr Harbinson you do not know

John Hart i do not think so

Mr Harbinson how many women refused to leave their berths

John Hart several

Mr Harbinson could you give us any estimate

John Hart i might if i think

Commissioner his estimate in such circumstances is to my mind of no value at all

Mr Harbinson was it a small number compared with the number that came up with you

John Hart oh yes

Mr Harbinson a very small number

John Hart yes

Mr Harbinson you have told us – i think – that there were sixty third-class stewards

John Hart yes

Mr Harbinson how many of these sixty were in the afterpart of the ship

John Hart none

Mr Harbinson can you tell us how many were in the after and how many were in the forward part

John Hart no

Mr Harbinson could you give us any estimate of the number of women and children who were in the afterpart of the ship – third-class men women and children

John Hart no

Mr Harbinson you can give us no estimate of the numbers of the third-class passengers who were in the after portion

John Hart no

Mr Harbinson and therefore you cannot tell me how many stewards were allotted to look after the third-class passengers

John Hart in the afterpart of the ship i can

Mr Harbinson that is what i am asking you

John Hart eight

Mr Harbinson eight stewards to look after all the third-class passengers in that portion

John Hart that is for the sleeping accommodation

Mr Harbinson it is a considerable distance is it not from the aft part of the ship to the boat deck

John Hart yes

Mr Harbinson you have told us that you saw a number of stewards placed at various portions to direct the third-class passengers how they were to go

John Hart yes

Mr Harbinson about how many were so placed

John Hart i passed about five or six on the starboard side

Mr Harbinson who else besides you then were bringing people up from their berths – rousing them and bringing them up to the boat deck – how many others

John Hart almost eight – a portion of the third-class stewards were room stewards – of whom i am the only survivor

Mr Harbinson i understand that there were only eight third-class stewards in the aft portion altogether

John Hart to look after them

Mr Harbinson who were stationed at various places to direct the third-class passengers the way they were to go

John Hart not of that eight

Mr Harbinson there were five

John Hart five others

Mr Harbinson what class stewards were they

John Hart i could not tell you – stewards were placed all round the ship

Mr Harbinson do you know who placed them there

John Hart i cannot tell you

Mr Harbinson do you know the stewards by sight who were placed to direct the third-class passengers

John Hart no

Mr Harbinson would it be right if anyone said that a number of sailors were keeping back the third-class passengers from reaching the boat deck

John Hart would it be right to do so

Mr Harbinson would it be right if anyone said so

John Hart i do not say that it would be right

Mr Harbinson i asked you would it be right if anyone said so

John Hart i would not like to say it would be right

Commissioner would it be true

John Hart i should not think so

Mr Harbinson it is not what you think – did you see any sailors keeping back the third-class passengers from reaching the boat deck

Commissioner did you see anyone keeping the third-class passengers back – so as to prevent them from getting to the boat deck

John Hart no my lord

Mr Harbinson you told us about a rush of men from the front part of the ship coming aft

John Hart yes

Mr Harbinson they were coming towards the third-class quarters

John Hart yes

Mr Harbinson they were third-class passengers

John Hart they were

Mr Harbinson why do you think they were coming aft

John Hart because i saw them coming aft

Mr Harbinson i quite realise that you saw them – but what was it caused them do you think to do that – was it because they could not escape to the boat deck by the companion ladder leading to the front part of the ship

John Hart i do not believe so

Commissioner how can he know that – do let us have some sort of order in these questions – how can he know why they did come aft

Mr Harbinson did you form any opinion at the time

Commissioner did you ask them why they were coming aft

John Hart no sir there was no occasion to ask

Mr Harbinson did you form any opinion at the time

John Hart i knew why they were coming aft

Mr Harbinson that is what i want to know – why did they come aft

John Hart because the forward section had already taken water

Mr Harbinson and that was the only way they could escape

John Hart not necessarily no – they could escape from the fore part of the ship

Mr Harbinson up the companion ladder would have been the nearest way for them would it not

John Hart yes

Mr Harbinson but they did not do that – they chose the other way

John Hart they chose the other way

Mr Harbinson that is rather curious is it not

John Hart no it is not curious at all

Mr Harbinson is it not

John Hart no

Mr Harbinson that is to say – they go the whole length of the ship and come up from the well deck at the back – rather than go up the companion ladder leading from the fore deck to the boat deck

John Hart perhaps the people did not stop to think where they were going

Mr Harbinson if there had been anybody to show them they would not have had occasion to think

John Hart that may be so

Mr Harbinson according to you all the women and children from the aft part of the boat who were taken up and who wanted to escape could have done so

John Hart i do not doubt that for a moment

Mr Harbinson can you explain how it was – that being so – that fifty-five per cent of the women of the third class were drowned

John Hart i cannot account for it no sir

Mr Harbinson i would like you to try and give us your opinion – that is a very high percentage is it not

John Hart i simply referred to those that i took up

Commissioner were you ever in an accident like this before

John Hart something similar my lord

Mr Harbinson when was that – were a great many people drowned

John Hart there was nobody drowned

Mr Harbinson then it was not an accident – can you form any opinion as to what percentage of third-class passengers might be expected to be drowned in an accident like this

John Hart no – my lord

Commissioner do not ask him such questions they do not help me at all

Mr Harbinson if i may respectfully explain to your lordship – after what he has said it raises a curious condition of affairs – that all the women could have escaped that wanted to escape – and yet the fact remains as stated by the learned attorney general that the percentage of the third-class female passengers who were drowned was fifty-five

Commissioner i know but you are wasting our time by asking a steward questions about percentages – he does not know anything about such things – ask him about things that happened and that he saw and that he can tell us of – and then we will form our own opinion as to what deductions are to be drawn from the facts

Mr Harbinson i do not think i shall ask him anything more my lord

Mr Harbinson sits.

Commissioner do you want to ask this witness any more questions

The Solicitor General stands.

Solicitor General just one or two my lord – (*To Witness.*) some questions have been put to you by some of these gentlemen rather suggesting that you discouraged these third-class people from doing what was best to save their lives – did you do anything of the sort

John Hart no sir i would not take it that way

Solicitor General i suppose you found they got a little excited when they were asked to put their lifebelts on

John Hart they were simply told to put their lifebelts on in a quiet manner to prevent any kind of panic that might have ensued

Solicitor General and you did your best to discharge that duty

John Hart yes

Solicitor General was that before any order had been passed along that these people were to go up to the boat deck

John Hart yes

Solicitor General and when the order was passed along that they were to be taken up to the boat deck did you do your best to get them through

John Hart i did my duty sir – to get them through

The Solicitor General sits.

Clerk the witness withdraws

George Symons enters.

Clerk day ten – george symons – lookout on the titanic – the attorney general

The Attorney General stands.

Attorney General when you saw the titanic go down did you hear any cries from the people that went down with the boat

George Symons yes

Attorney General did you try to rescue them

George Symons i thought at the time – being master of the situation – it was not safe to go back at that time

Attorney General let us understand that – you heard cries

George Symons yes

Attorney General and cries which you knew were of persons in distress

George Symons quite so

Attorney General if you could have reached any one of those persons you could have saved the life of that person

George Symons yes – but i thought at the time – by using my own discretion – that it was not safe in any way to have gone back to that ship as she disappeared

Attorney General do you tell my lord that you determined – without consultation with anybody – that you would not go back

George Symons i determined by my own wish – as i was master of the situation – to go back when i thought that most of the danger was over

Attorney General what

George Symons i used my own discretion – as being master of the situation at the time – that it was not safe to have gone back at that time until everything was over

Commissioner i want to know why – what was it that you were afraid of

George Symons i was not afraid of anything – i was only afraid of endangering the lives of the people i had in the boat

Commissioner how – what was the danger – the ship had gone to the bottom she was no longer a danger – what were you afraid of

George Symons at that time the ship had only just disappeared

Commissioner never mind – it had disappeared – and gone to the bottom – two miles down or something like that – what were you afraid of

George Symons i was afraid of swarming

Commissioner of what

George Symons of the swarming of people – swamping the boat

Commissioner that is it – that is what you were afraid of – you were afraid there were too many people in the water

George Symons yes

Commissioner and that your boat would be swamped

George Symons yes

Commissioner i am not satisfied at all

Attorney General now i want to know a little more about that – was the question raised about your going back to the people who were shrieking at this time

George Symons none whatever

Attorney General you mean nothing was said – either by you or anybody

George Symons i used my own discretion

Attorney General you have told us that several times –
i understand that – you used your discretion – and that –
you were master of the situation – we got those phrases –
what i am asking you about now is whether at that time
you heard anything said by anybody on the boat about
going back

George Symons none whatever

Attorney General either by you or by any of the crew

George Symons no

Attorney General or by any of the passengers

George Symons no

Attorney General then if i understand correctly what
you say – your story to my lord is – the vessel had gone
down – there were people in the water shrieking for help –
you were in the boat with plenty of room – nobody ever
mentioned going back – nobody ever said a word about
it – you just simply lay on your oars – is that the story
you want my lord to believe

George Symons yes – that is the story

Attorney General did you know sir cosmo duff gordon
before he got into that boat

George Symons no sir

Attorney General did you hear anybody in the boat say
that you ought to go back to try and save some of the
people

George Symons no

Attorney General did you hear anybody talking in the
boat at all at this time

George Symons no

Attorney General did you hear one of the passengers say that it would be too dangerous to go back

George Symons no sir – i heard nothing

Attorney General that you might get swamped

George Symons no – i heard nothing

Attorney General that was your view – that it was too dangerous to go back because you might get swamped

George Symons yes

Attorney General that is what you thought

George Symons that was my own view – yes

Attorney General did you hear anybody express that same view

George Symons no

Attorney General since – have you discussed it since

George Symons no

Attorney General has any lawyer seen you about your evidence

George Symons i have given evidence in two or three places

Attorney General were you asked to make a statement to somebody representing sir cosmo and lady duff gordon

George Symons well – i was asked to make a statement and i just simply told the truth

Attorney General were you asked to make a statement by somebody on behalf of sir cosmo and lady duff gordon

George Symons yes they did say they were representing sir cosmo duff gordon

Attorney General when was it that somebody came to see you on their behalf

George Symons it must have been on tuesday evening

Attorney General was it a gentleman

George Symons i beg your pardon

Attorney General was it a gentleman – a man – who came to see you

George Symons it was a gentleman

Attorney General two men

George Symons a gentleman

Commissioner did you know he was coming – had they written to you to say he was coming

George Symons i just knew that there was a gentleman coming but i did not know who he was

Commissioner how did you know that there was a gentleman coming

George Symons how did i know – the message was brought to my house that someone was coming to see me

Commissioner who brought the message

George Symons by telephone

Commissioner did you ask through the telephone who he was

George Symons i never had nothing to do with the telephone whatsoever

Attorney General had you communicated with sir cosmo and lady duff gordon since your return

George Symons no – i communicated with no one

Commissioner do you happen to know the name of the gentleman that came to see you

George Symons no i do not

Commissioner you never asked his name

George Symons i never asked the gentleman's name

Commissioner have you seen him since

George Symons no

Attorney General how long was he with you

George Symons i suppose roughly it might have been an hour or it might have been a little more

Commissioner he took down what you said i suppose in writing

George Symons that i could not say sir what he was doing of

Attorney General was he writing when you were there

George Symons he just wrote down a little but what he was doing of i could not say – i never said much i simply stated the truth and that is all

Attorney General did you sign any statement at this interview

George Symons yes i signed my name

Attorney General what happened to the statement

George Symons that i cannot say

Attorney General was it taken away by this gentleman

George Symons yes

Attorney General were you asked whether you were – master of the situation

George Symons oh yes sir i was asked that

Attorney General that is what the gentleman said to you

George Symons yes

Attorney General the gentleman asked you – were you master of the situation – and i suppose you said yes

George Symons certainly sir

Attorney General were you asked whether you – exercised your discretion

George Symons how do you mean exercised my discretion

Attorney General that was your expression today – it is not mine – did the gentleman say to you – did you exercise your discretion

George Symons is that for me to say in court here

Attorney General i am asking you

George Symons i know you are asking me but is that for me to say

Attorney General whether the gentleman asked you that

George Symons whether the gentleman asked me that

Attorney General why should you be so shy about it

George Symons i am not shy at all about it

Attorney General why do you want the protection of the court – why don't you answer the question

George Symons you put the question to me and i told you – the master of the situation

Attorney General just follow what i am putting to you – you say a gentleman was there with you

George Symons yes

Attorney General and he put questions to you

George Symons yes

Attorney General i am asking you did he put this question to you – did you exercise your discretion as to whether you should go back or not

George Symons i told him yes

Commissioner then he did ask you the question and you said yes

Attorney General did the gentleman tell you that you ought not to say anything about this

George Symons the gentleman said nothing whatsoever to me sir

Attorney General i do not quite understand why you should have objected to answering the question i put to you

George Symons i think myself sir like this – i do not know who the gentleman was neither did i altogether at the time – and it was in my own private home – and i think myself it was not a case to be put before the court

Attorney General do not drop your voice – you thought it was not a case to be put before the court

George Symons not that question you put then

Attorney General but why not

George Symons i have answered it now so that it has gone

Attorney General i would like to understand why it is that you think that question ought not to be put to you – what is your objection to it

George Symons i think myself sir that what you do in your own private life is no business of no one – that is what i think and that is a sailor's view of it

Attorney General so that you thought that this conversation between you and this gentleman representing sir cosmo and lady duff gordon ought to be treated as private

George Symons it was no business of nobody's

Attorney General neither of the courts nor of anybody else

George Symons not in that regard no – because there was nothing more than i just simply stated the outline of the thing

Attorney General a brief outline of the story

George Symons yes

Attorney General how long did it take you to give that brief outline

George Symons just over an hour i suppose

Attorney General he put questions to you

George Symons no – he may have put one or two now and then

Attorney General you told me about the exercise of your discretion and your being master of the situation – those you have told me about

George Symons yes

Attorney General did you say anything to him about having received any money from sir cosmo duff gordon – do speak up

George Symons i was just thinking whether i said anything – i will not tell a lie

Attorney General i say it does not want much thinking about to recollect that you had the money

George Symons that is right enough but i am thinking whether i mentioned it to the man – it is no use me telling you a lie – i was just thinking whether i said it

Commissioner now think – and tell us what the answer is

George Symons yes i did tell him – i told him at the time it was given me it was a surprise

Commissioner a surprise

George Symons yes it was a great surprise to me when i received it

Attorney General that is what you told him

George Symons yes

Attorney General how much did you have

George Symons is that a question to submit sir

Commissioner yes

George Symons five pounds

Attorney General have you had any more since

George Symons no none whatever

Attorney General when did you have that

George Symons about a day – it may have been two – before we arrived in new york on the carpathia

Attorney General did you hear sir cosmo duff gordon say anything in the boat

George Symons no sir i heard sir cosmo say nothing

Attorney General how many hours were you in the boat before you were picked up by the carpathia

George Symons it must have been five or more

Attorney General did you hear any of the crew say anything

George Symons no sir – they only gave a bit of a cheer when they sighted the carpathia first

Attorney General are we to understand from you that during the whole time you were in the boat nothing was ever said until a cheer was raised when you saw the carpathia

George Symons there may have been a conversation among themselves but i heard nothing

Attorney General were not you surprised that nobody suggested that you should go back to pick up the people who were drowning

George Symons yes

Commissioner you were surprised

George Symons i expected fully for someone to say something about it

Commissioner that seemed reasonable

George Symons yes that seemed reasonable sir

Commissioner but you would not have thought it reasonable if they had said it

George Symons not at the time no sir

Attorney General you have thought about it a good deal since

George Symons yes

Attorney General you have realised that if you had gone back you might have saved a good many people

George Symons quite so

The Attorney General sits.

Mr Scanlon stands.

Mr Scanlon i suppose you knew that the titanic had over thirteen hundred passengers

George Symons oh yes – i do not know the exact numbers of course

Mr Scanlon and eight hundred and ninety-two of a crew – that altogether you had on board over two thousand two hundred people

George Symons i do not know the exact numbers of course

Mr Scanlon did you realise that you had not lifeboat accommodation for half the people you had on the boat

George Symons yes

Mr Scanlon you knew that

George Symons yes

Mr Scanlon your boat corresponds exactly to the boat on the opposite side – to emergency boat number two

George Symons yes

Mr Scanlon do you know that number two boat took off twenty-three to twenty-five passengers – chiefly women – did you know that

George Symons no sir i did not know that

Mr Scanlon can you explain to my lord how it is that this order was given for your boat to go away with only five passengers

George Symons i cannot say sir

Mr Scanlon it is your evidence that there were no passengers either male or female on the deck

George Symons i saw none

Mr Scanlon knowing that you had not got accommodation for all the passengers you must have known and realised that there were plenty of passengers left behind in the ship – the titanic

George Symons yes

Mr Scanlon the sea was calm

George Symons yes

Mr Scanlon and the night was calm

George Symons yes

Mr Scanlon the conditions could not have been more favourable for rescuing people

George Symons no

Mr Scanlon did you attribute to cowardice the fact that your passengers did not all ask you to go back

George Symons no sir i never had a thought in my head of cowardice

Mr Scanlon looking back on the whole situation – and considering that you had a boat practically empty – with only five passengers and accommodation for fifteen or twenty more – was it not cowardice that prevented the passengers and the crew from going back

George Symons no i cannot see that

Mr Scanlon can you give any other account – can you account for it in any other way except by the exercise of what you are pleased to call your discretion

George Symons that is right sir – that is the only thing i can see

Mr Scanlon you admit it was cowardly

George Symons no i do not admit it was cowardly

Mr Scanlon is not a seaman – when the passengers in his boat are in danger – expected to run risks in order to save life

George Symons quite so

Commissioner this is mere argument mr scanlon

Mr Scanlon i shall not press it further my lord

Commissioner have a little mercy on the man

Mr Scanlon sits.

Clerk the witness withdraws

Sir Cosmo Duff Gordon enters.

Clerk day ten – sir cosmo duff gordon – first-class passenger on the titanic – the attorney general

The Attorney General stands.

Attorney General did you hear any orders given with reference to number one boat

Sir Cosmo Duff Gordon yes – an officer – i don't know who he was – ordered . . .

Attorney General an officer

Sir Cosmo Duff Gordon yes i think it was the same officer who had been doing the other boats – we had followed them along – he said – man the emergency boat – and he said so to a number of i think firemen or some of the crew – some eight or ten of them who were standing there – i then spoke to him and i said – may we get into the boat – and he said – yes i wish you would – or – very glad if you would – or something like that – there were no passengers at all near us then – he put the ladies in and helped me in myself and we were joined by two americans who came running along the deck – i think he then told two other or three other of the firemen that they might just as well get in – and then he put one man – i did not know his name until lately – in charge of the boat – symons

Attorney General can you give us any explanation why it was that this boat was lowered away with so few people in it when there were so many people left on the ship which was in danger

Sir Cosmo Duff Gordon there were no people visible i am quite sure of that when i got into the boat

Commissioner but there were many people close at hand

Sir Cosmo Duff Gordon i do not know – there was no one visible certainly

Attorney General you had noticed that other boats had been filled with as many people as they could possibly carry

Sir Cosmo Duff Gordon i presume so – i had not noticed very much – but there were no more to go – i am trying to say there were no more on that particular part – on that side of the deck anyway there were no more in view

Attorney General when you got into the boat and the men started rowing away from the vessel – as we know they did – how far do you think that your boat had got before the titanic went down

Sir Cosmo Duff Gordon well i have always said a thousand yards when telling anybody – but it is true i have only one eye and i am therefore presumed not to be a judge of distance – but i still think it

Attorney General did they continue rowing without stopping for what you consider a thousand yards distance

Sir Cosmo Duff Gordon no i think they rowed for two hundred yards or so and stopped – and then they rowed again i daresay another hundred or two hundred yards and stopped again and so on

Attorney General according to the account we have had it was certainly somewhere about that time – whatever the distance was – that the titanic went down

Sir Cosmo Duff Gordon yes

Attorney General did you hear cries

Sir Cosmo Duff Gordon yes – i heard the first explosion and i heard – i will not say the cries but a wail – one confused sound

Attorney General we do not want unnecessarily to prolong the discussion of it – but – they were the cries of people who were drowning

Sir Cosmo Duff Gordon yes

Attorney General there is no doubt about that

Sir Cosmo Duff Gordon yes i think so without doubt

Attorney General did it occur to you that with the room in your boat – if you could get to these people – you could save some

Sir Cosmo Duff Gordon it is difficult to say what occurred to me – again – i was minding my wife and we were in a rather abnormal condition you know – there were many things to think about – but of course it quite well occurred to one that people in the water could be saved by a boat – yes

Attorney General and did you hear a suggestion made that you should go back – that your boat should go back to the place whence the cries came

Sir Cosmo Duff Gordon no i did not

Attorney General do you mean that you never heard that at all

Sir Cosmo Duff Gordon i heard no suggestion of going back

Attorney General was any notice taken of those cries in your boat

Sir Cosmo Duff Gordon i think the men began to row away again immediately

Attorney General did they get any orders to do that

Sir Cosmo Duff Gordon that i could not say

Attorney General that would seem rather strange would it not

Sir Cosmo Duff Gordon no

Commissioner to row away from the cries

Sir Cosmo Duff Gordon to row – i do not know which way they were rowing – but i think they began to row – in my opinion it was to stop the sound

Attorney General these cries continued for some time did they not

Sir Cosmo Duff Gordon i said the men began to row very soon after the cries were first heard

Attorney General but the cries continued for some time

Sir Cosmo Duff Gordon yes i believe they did

Attorney General as the men proceeded to row away did the cries sound fainter

Sir Cosmo Duff Gordon oh you could not hear the sound at all when the men were rowing

Attorney General does that mean that in your boat they were not rowing when you heard the cries

Sir Cosmo Duff Gordon the moment the titanic sank of course everything stopped – there was a dead silence

Attorney General and then you of course did hear the cries

Sir Cosmo Duff Gordon yes – then we did

Attorney General you mean you continued to hear the cries until the men started rowing again

Sir Cosmo Duff Gordon yes which was very soon – immediately almost

Attorney General we have heard from two witnesses that a suggestion was made that your boat should go back to try to save some of the people

Sir Cosmo Duff Gordon yes

Attorney General what do you say about that

Sir Cosmo Duff Gordon i can only say i did not hear any suggestion – that is all i can say

Attorney General and you know it has been further said that one of the ladies – identified by the last witness as your wife – was afraid to go back because she thought you would be swamped

Sir Cosmo Duff Gordon i heard that

Attorney General did you hear your wife say that

Sir Cosmo Duff Gordon no

Attorney General or any lady

Sir Cosmo Duff Gordon no

Attorney General or any person

Sir Cosmo Duff Gordon no

Attorney General do you mean it might have happened but that you do not remember anything about it – or do you mean that it did not take place

Sir Cosmo Duff Gordon in my opinion it did not take place

Attorney General do you mean it is not true what the men are saying

Sir Cosmo Duff Gordon it comes to that of course

Attorney General i must ask you about the money – had you made any promise of a present to the men in the boat

Sir Cosmo Duff Gordon yes i did

Attorney General will you tell us about that

Sir Cosmo Duff Gordon i will – if i may i will tell you what happened

Attorney General yes

Sir Cosmo Duff Gordon there was a man sitting next to me – and of course in the dark i could see nothing of him – i never did see him and i do not know yet who he is – i suppose it would be some time when they rested on their oars – twenty minutes or half an hour after the titanic had sunk – a man said to me – i suppose you have lost everything – and i said – of course – he says – but you can get some more – and i said – yes – well – he said – we have lost all our kit and the company won't give us any more and what is more our pay stops from tonight – all they will do is send us back to london – so i said to him – you fellows need not worry about that i will give you a fiver each to start a new kit – that is the whole of that five-pound note story

Clerk the witness withdraws – there will now be a short adjournment

End of Act One.

Act Two

The stage is as before.

Clerk proceedings will now resume – day eleven – sir cosmo duff gordon

Mr Harbinson stands.

Mr Harbinson did i rightly understand you on friday to say that about twenty minutes after the titanic sank – while you were in the boat – was the time when the conversation with reference to the presents took place

Sir Cosmo Duff Gordon something of that sort – twenty minutes or half an hour i should fancy

Mr Harbinson that was while those scenes – which we have heard described so often to us – took place – and harrowing cries could distinctly be heard by you

Sir Cosmo Duff Gordon oh no

Commissioner why do you assume that

Mr Harbinson i will put it in the form of a question – was it

Commissioner there is no evidence to that effect – it is very irregular to assume facts that are not proved

Mr Harbinson at question 12586 sir cosmo duff gordon says – i suppose it would be some time when they rested on their oars – twenty minutes or half an hour after the titanic had sunk a man said to me – i suppose you have lost everything

Commissioner yes but consider the gloss you put upon the thing – you say that this conversation was taking place while the cries were still being heard – now where is the statement to that effect

Mr Harbinson it is in evidence that they heard the cries twenty minutes after the titanic sank – there is evidence that the cries lasted for an hour and a half – and if they did they were audible twenty minutes afterwards

Commissioner where is that

Mr Harbinson one of the witnesses on friday

Commissioner i am talking about this witness – your duty is to assist me

Mr Harbinson yes i am anxious to do so

Commissioner not to try to make out a case for this class or that class or another class – but to assist me in arriving at the truth – and you do not do it by trying to make out a case against one person or another – it does not help me a bit

Mr Harbinson i understand my lord – (*To Witness.*) did you hear the cries twenty minutes after the titanic sank

Sir Cosmo Duff Gordon no i cannot tell you at all about that

Mr Harbinson you cannot remember

Sir Cosmo Duff Gordon i do not think anything like that

Mr Harbinson you do not

Sir Cosmo Duff Gordon i do not think so – i cannot say – the men were rowing a great deal

Mr Harbinson did you tell them to row to drown the cries

Sir Cosmo Duff Gordon no

Mr Harbinson was not this rather an exceptional time – twenty minutes after the titanic sank – to make suggestions in the boat about giving away five-pound notes

Sir Cosmo Duff Gordon no i think not – it was a most natural time – everything was quiet – the men had stopped rowing – the men were quite quiet lying on their oars doing nothing for some time – and then the ship having gone i think it was a natural enough remark for a man to make to me – i suppose you have lost everything

Mr Harbinson would it not have been more in harmony with the traditions of seamanship that that should have been the time that you should have suggested to the sailors to have gone and tried if they could rescue anyone

Sir Cosmo Duff Gordon i have said that i did not consider the possibility – or rather i should put it the possibility of being able to help anybody never occurred to me at all

Mr Harbinson that is to say – would i accurately state your position if i summed it up this way – that you considered when you were safe yourselves that all the others might perish

Sir Cosmo Duff Gordon no that is not quite the way to put it

Commissioner do you think a question of that kind is fair to the witness – the witness's position is bad enough – do you think it is fair to put a question of that kind to him – i do not

Mr Harbinson if your lordship says so i will not pursue it any further – (*To Witness.*) had you heard the officer who was in control at the time number one boat was lowered give instructions that the boat should remain within a certain distance of the sinking liner

Sir Cosmo Duff Gordon no i did not hear that – i said so i think

Mr Harbinson did you hear any instructions given in the boat as to the direction the boat should take

Sir Cosmo Duff Gordon in what boat

Mr Harbinson the emergency boat

Sir Cosmo Duff Gordon did i hear it in the emergency boat

Mr Harbinson yes

Sir Cosmo Duff Gordon no i heard no instructions at all – by whom

Mr Harbinson by any person

Sir Cosmo Duff Gordon in the boat

Mr Harbinson yes

Sir Cosmo Duff Gordon no

Mr Harbinson did you hear any suggestions made

Sir Cosmo Duff Gordon what about

Mr Harbinson by any members of the crew or any of the passengers in the emergency boat to the coxswain as to the direction the boat should take

Sir Cosmo Duff Gordon no i do not think i did – there was one man – one of the passengers called out two or three times – let us go that way let us go the other – but i do not think any notice was taken of it

Mr Harbinson was any reply made to that man when it was suggested going in a particular way

Sir Cosmo Duff Gordon no i think no notice was taken

Mr Harbinson did you hear anything said

Sir Cosmo Duff Gordon no

Mr Harbinson you said nothing

Sir Cosmo Duff Gordon no i said nothing – how do you mean i said nothing

Mr Harbinson did you give no answer

Sir Cosmo Duff Gordon it was going on all night – it was not once he said it

Mr Harbinson was an instruction given or did you hear anything said shortly after the titanic went down

Sir Cosmo Duff Gordon no i do not think anything was said then

Mr Harbinson was it an answer to this suggestion of his as to the direction in which the boat should go that you said – i will give you a fiver

Sir Cosmo Duff Gordon i really do not understand your question – you must put it plainly

Mr Harbinson yes i will put it quite distinctly – an instruction – or rather an observation was made by someone – that the emergency boat should go in a particular direction – is not that so

Sir Cosmo Duff Gordon that was going on all the latter part of the night by this man – yes – continually

Mr Harbinson before the titanic went down

Sir Cosmo Duff Gordon no no no

Mr Harbinson after the titanic went down

Sir Cosmo Duff Gordon yes – i really do not know – it seemed to be most of the time – he called boat ahoy and so on

Mr Harbinson the question i put to you is this – when you first heard this observation made with reference to

the direction in which this emergency boat should go –
was it then – twenty minutes after the titanic sank – that
you suggested that you would give them a fiver each

Sir Cosmo Duff Gordon no – i see what you mean – no it
was not – not in any connection with it – the man calling
out to go this way and that had no effect i think on
anybody – nor on this subject at all – it had nothing to
do with it

Commissioner if you will put your question plainly it
would perhaps be understood better – your question – as
i understand it – really is this – did you promise a five-
pound note in order to induce the men in the boat to row
away from the drowning people – that is what you want
to ask

Mr Harbinson that is the effect of it

Commissioner well why do you not put it in plain words

Mr Harbinson sits.

The Attorney General stands.

Attorney General one matter i want to ask you about –
you heard a passenger talking – giving directions in the
boat

Sir Cosmo Duff Gordon well he was not giving directions
but he was saying – let us go here and boat ahoy

Attorney General was there any conversation between
him and you as to which way you should go

Sir Cosmo Duff Gordon no there was only one remark i
made to him

Attorney General what was that

Sir Cosmo Duff Gordon to ask him to be quiet

Attorney General was that mr stengel

Sir Cosmo Duff Gordon is it necessary to say who

Attorney General well it is necessary if you can – i do not know why you should not – if you can tell us – can you tell us

Sir Cosmo Duff Gordon i can perfectly

Attorney General well who was it

Sir Cosmo Duff Gordon yes it was he

Attorney General i asked you because i see he has been examined in america – and i want to call your attention to this statement of his – i am reading from the 30th april at page 14 of the inquiry before the senate commission – do you know who gave directions – answer – i think between sir duff gordon and myself we decided which way to go – that is what mr stengel said

Sir Cosmo Duff Gordon i think it is wrong

Attorney General what

Sir Cosmo Duff Gordon it is not the case – there was no question at all – i never spoke to the coxswain in any way to give him any directions

Attorney General that is all i want to ask you

The Attorney General sits.

Clerk the witness withdraws

Lady Duff Gordon enters.

Clerk day eleven – lady duff gordon – first-class passenger on the titanic – the attorney general

The Attorney General stands.

Attorney General lady duff gordon will you remember on the night of this disaster to the titanic you were wakened i think by the collision

Lady Duff Gordon i was

Attorney General i only want you to tell me one thing before we get to the boat – had there been offers to you to go into any of the lifeboats

Lady Duff Gordon oh yes they came and tried to drag me away

Attorney General you mean some of the sailors

Lady Duff Gordon the sailors – i was holding my husband's arm – they were very anxious that i should go

Attorney General and you refused to go

Lady Duff Gordon absolutely

Attorney General well eventually you did go with your husband as we know in what has been called the emergency boat

Lady Duff Gordon yes i did

Attorney General just tell us quite shortly – i do not want to go into it in any detail – but quite shortly how it was you went into that boat – do you remember

Lady Duff Gordon oh quite well

Attorney General well would you tell my lord

Lady Duff Gordon after the three boats had gone down my husband miss franks and myself were left standing on the deck – there were no other people on the deck at all visible and i had quite made up my mind that i was going to be drowned – and then suddenly there was this little boat in front of us – this little thing – (*Pointing to model.*) – and we saw some sailors and an officer apparently giving them orders and i said to my husband – ought we not to be doing something – he said – oh we must wait for orders – and we stood there for quite some time while these men were fixing things up – and then my husband went forward and said – might we get into this boat – and the officer said in a very polite way indeed – oh certainly do i will be very pleased – then somebody hitched me up from the deck and pitched me into the boat and then i think miss franks was pitched in – it was not a case of getting in at all – we could not have got in it was quite high – they pitched us up in the sort of way – (*Indicating.*) into the boat and after we had been in a little while the boat was started to be lowered and one american gentleman got pitched in – and one american gentleman was pitched in while the boat was being lowered down

Attorney General now you will remember when you got into the boat – and before the titanic sank – did the men start rowing away from the titanic

Lady Duff Gordon oh the moment we touched the water the men started rowing

Attorney General had you heard any orders given

Lady Duff Gordon yes

Attorney General do you remember what they were

Lady Duff Gordon as far as i can remember it was row quickly away from the boat for about two hundred yards

Attorney General and come back if called upon

Lady Duff Gordon no

Attorney General you did not hear that

Lady Duff Gordon oh no

Attorney General i do not quite understand

Lady Duff Gordon i did not hear that

Attorney General you did not hear it

Lady Duff Gordon no

Attorney General as far as you know all they had to do was to row out two hundred yards

Lady Duff Gordon yes

Attorney General then did the men commence doing that

Lady Duff Gordon at once

Attorney General and did you hear any conversation at all in the boat before the titanic sank

Lady Duff Gordon no

Attorney General do you understand the question i was putting to you

Lady Duff Gordon no i did not hear it in our little boat

Attorney General yes

Lady Duff Gordon no

Attorney General let me ask you again – i am speaking to you of before the titanic sank – you understand

Lady Duff Gordon yes

Attorney General what i am asking you is – before she sank did you hear the men saying anything in the boat

Lady Duff Gordon no

Attorney General did you hear anything said about suction

Lady Duff Gordon well perhaps i may have heard it – but i was terribly sick and i could not swear to it

Attorney General what

Lady Duff Gordon i was awfully sick – i do not think i could swear to it

Attorney General i am asking you about something which i understand you have said quite recently

Commissioner read it to her

Lady Duff Gordon yes will you please

Attorney General i am asking you about something which i only know from your statement to your solicitor – did you hear a voice say – let us get away

Lady Duff Gordon yes i think so

Attorney General did you hear it said – it is such an enormous boat none of us know what the suction may be if she is a goner

Lady Duff Gordon yes i heard them speaking of the enormous boat – it was the word suction i was not sure of – i see what you mean

Attorney General it is not what i mean – lady duff gordon – it is what you are said to have said to your solicitor

Lady Duff Gordon well i may have said so

Attorney General such an enormous boat – that is referring to the titanic

Lady Duff Gordon yes

Attorney General none of us know what the suction may be if she is a goner

Lady Duff Gordon that was – i am sure – long before the titanic sank

Attorney General that is what i am asking you

Lady Duff Gordon yes

Attorney General i put it to you but i do not think you appreciated the question

Lady Duff Gordon no i did not

Attorney General it was before the titanic sank

Lady Duff Gordon yes it was before

Attorney General now after the titanic sank you still continued to be seasick i understand

Lady Duff Gordon yes terribly

Attorney General i only want to ask you one question about that – tell me first of all do you recollect very well what happened when you were in the boat

Lady Duff Gordon no

Attorney General your mind is hazy about it

Lady Duff Gordon very

Attorney General there may have been some talk which you would not recollect i suppose

Lady Duff Gordon well i do not know

Attorney General you think you might

Lady Duff Gordon i think i would

Attorney General i will put to you definitely what is said with reference to yourself – did you hear after the titanic had sunk the cries of the people who were drowning

Lady Duff Gordon no – after the titanic sank i never heard a cry

Attorney General you never heard anything

Lady Duff Gordon no not after the titanic sank

Attorney General did not you hear cries at all

Lady Duff Gordon yes before she sank – terrible cries

Attorney General before she sank

Lady Duff Gordon yes

Attorney General did you see her sink

Lady Duff Gordon i did

Attorney General you mean you heard nothing at all after that

Lady Duff Gordon my impression was that there was absolute silence

Attorney General were the men rowing

Lady Duff Gordon yes

Attorney General what – all the time

Lady Duff Gordon no they began to row as soon as the boat went down

Attorney General did you hear a proposal made that you should go back to where the titanic was sunk

Lady Duff Gordon no

Attorney General did you hear any shouting in your boat – it would be better if you would attend to me

Lady Duff Gordon i am listening

Attorney General did you hear anybody shout out in the boat that you ought to go back

Lady Duff Gordon no

Attorney General with the object of saving people who were in the titanic

Lady Duff Gordon no

Attorney General you knew there were people in the titanic did you not

Lady Duff Gordon no i did not think so – i do not think i was thinking anything about it

Attorney General did you say that it would be dangerous to go back that you might get swamped

Lady Duff Gordon no

The Attorney General sits.

Mr Scanlon i have no questions

Mr Harbinson i do not wish to ask anything

Clerk the witness withdraws

Charles Lightoller enters.

Clerk days twelve and fourteen – charles lightoller – second officer on the titanic – the solicitor general

The Solicitor General stands.

Solicitor General you are mr charles herbert lightoller i think

Charles Lightoller yes

Solicitor General were you second officer on the titanic

Charles Lightoller i was

Solicitor General i think you hold a master's certificate

Charles Lightoller yes

Solicitor General you passed for master in 1899

Charles Lightoller about that yes

Solicitor General and do you also hold an extra master's certificate

Charles Lightoller yes

Solicitor General which you passed for in 1902

Charles Lightoller yes

Solicitor General how long have you been in the white star company's employ

Charles Lightoller nearly twelve and a half years

Solicitor General that would be since 1900

Charles Lightoller january 1900

Solicitor General sailing with that company across the atlantic many times is most of your experience in the north atlantic

Charles Lightoller most yes

Solicitor General just give me if you will the arrangement about the watches between the chief officer the first officer and yourself – i suppose you would count as the three senior officers

Charles Lightoller yes exactly

Solicitor General how was that

Charles Lightoller the chief officer had from two until six a.m. and p.m. – the second officer . . .

Solicitor General that is you

Charles Lightoller yes myself – the second officer relieved the chief at six o'clock and was on deck until ten – six to ten a.m. and p.m. – the first officer was on deck from ten to two a.m. and p.m.

Solicitor General and during your watch which extended from six till ten did she – the titanic – maintain the same speed – as far as you know

Charles Lightoller as far as i know

Solicitor General then who would be on the bridge – is it one or two junior officers would be on the bridge with you

Charles Lightoller two junior officers on watch at all times

Solicitor General there would be a quartermaster at the wheel

Charles Lightoller and a standby quartermaster

Solicitor General another quartermaster standing by

Charles Lightoller exactly

Solicitor General and there would be two lookout men in the crow's nest

Charles Lightoller at all times

Solicitor General and being on the bridge – and in charge – would it be your responsibility to determine any question about reduction of speed

Charles Lightoller if i thought it necessary i should advise the commander

Solicitor General but you thought the water was clear enough and you could see

Charles Lightoller perfectly clear

Solicitor General you have had great experience of the north atlantic at all times of the year – just tell me – when a liner is known to be approaching ice is it or is it not – in your experience – usual to reduce speed

Charles Lightoller i have never known speed to be reduced in any ship i have ever been in in the north atlantic in clear weather – not on account of ice

Solicitor General assuming that the weather is clear

Charles Lightoller clear

Solicitor General can you suggest at all how it can have come about that this iceberg should not have been seen at a greater distance

Charles Lightoller it is very difficult indeed to come to any conclusion – of course we know now the extraordinary combination of circumstances that existed at the time – which you would not meet again in a hundred years –

that they should all have existed just on that particular night shows of course – that everything was against us

Commissioner when you make a general statement of that kind i want you to particularise – what were the circumstances

Charles Lightoller i was going to give them my lord – in the first place there was no moon

Commissioner that is frequently the case

Charles Lightoller very– then there was no wind – not the slightest breath of air – and most particular of all in my estimation is the fact – a most extraordinary circumstance – that there was not any swell – had there been the slightest degree of swell i have no doubt that berg would have been seen in plenty of time to clear it

Commissioner wait a minute – no moon – no wind – no swell

Charles Lightoller the moon we knew of – the wind we knew of – but the absence of swell we did not know of – you naturally conclude that you do not meet with a sea like it was – like a table top or a floor – a most extraordinary circumstance – and i guarantee that ninety-nine men out of a hundred could never call to mind actual proof of there having been such an absolutely smooth sea

Commissioner but the swell got up later on

Charles Lightoller yes almost immediately – after i was in the water – i had not been on the raft – the upturned boat – more than half an hour or so – before a slight swell was distinctly noticeable

Commissioner we hear of one lady being very seasick

Charles Lightoller in the morning there was quite a breeze and we maintained our equilibrium with the greatest difficulty when the rough sea came towards us and before we got the lifeboat alongside the carpathia

Commissioner you were going to particularise the circumstances which you say combined to bring about the calamity – there was no moon no wind and no swell – is there anything else

Charles Lightoller the berg into which we must have run in my estimation must have been a berg which had very shortly before capsized – and that would leave most of it above the water practically black ice

Commissioner you think so

Charles Lightoller i think so or it must have been a berg broken from a glacier with the blue side towards us – but even in that case had it been a glacier there would still have been the white outline that captain smith spoke about – with a white outline – against no matter how dark a sky providing the stars are out and distinctly visible – you ought to pick it out in quite sufficient time to clear it at any time – that is to say providing the stars are out and providing it is not cloudy – you must remember that all the stars were out and there was not a cloud in the sky – so that at any rate there was bound to be a certain amount of reflected light – had it been field ice – had we been approaching field ice of more or less extent – looking down upon it it would have been very visible – you would have been able to see that field ice five miles away i should think – had it been a normal iceberg with three sides and the top white with just a glimpse of any of the white sides they would have shown sufficient reflected light to have been noticeable a mile and a half or two miles distant – the only way in which i can account for it is that this was probably a berg which had overturned as they most frequently do which had split and broken away – a berg will split into different divisions – into halves perhaps – and then it becomes top heavy and at the same time as it splits you have what are often spoken of as explosions and the berg will topple over – that brings most of the part that has been in the water above the water

Commissioner is there any other circumstance you wish to point out

Charles Lightoller no i think that is all

Commissioner just let us put that together – it is dark in the sense that there is no moon – with a bright starlight sky perfectly clear but there is no wind or swell – and if there had been there would have been some motion of the water against the bottom of the iceberg – which would have been noticeable

Charles Lightoller yes

Commissioner the iceberg in your opinion had probably quite recently turned turtle

Charles Lightoller yes

Commissioner and was displaying black ice with nothing white about it – that is it is it not

Charles Lightoller that is about it

Solicitor General supposing a ship in these circumstances did not go so fast through the water – would that make it less likely that these conditions would produce so serious an accident

Charles Lightoller of course if the ship was going slowly the impact would be less

Commissioner if the ship had been doing what the californian was doing – dead stopped – no calamity would have happened

Charles Lightoller no – had we seen the ice pack before we got into contact with the berg – or if we had seen one of the bigger bergs – or anything – except just happening to find that one particular berg

Solicitor General we have had evidence of the lookout man you know – and the lookout man says that – it was a dark mass that came through the haze and there was no white appearing until it came alongside the ship and that was just a fringe at the top – if an iceberg such as you have described has a black side and a white side it is just as likely that the black side is towards the ship as the other side

Charles Lightoller no – you see three sides and the top will be white and there is only one black side – if you take the end of a glacier which is protruding out of a valley or whatever it is there are two sides at the front and the top that are crystallised – and when it comes over the edge and breaks off short there is only this part at the back where it is broken away from the parent glacier which is black

Solicitor General do you mean that from whatever point you approached such an iceberg you ought to be able to see something white about it at a distance

Charles Lightoller yes

The Solicitor General sits.

Commissioner there is another question i want to ask you – the crow's nest man said that the berg appeared to come as it were out of a haze – is it possible that in the circumstances you have mentioned an iceberg might produce on the eyesight of these men the effect of a haze

Charles Lightoller it ought not to

Commissioner very well – that is quite sufficient

Mr Scanlon stands.

Mr Scanlon you are the senior officer of all the officers who have survived the titanic disaster

Charles Lightoller yes

Mr Scanlon what i want to suggest to you is that it was recklessness – utter recklessness – in view of the conditions which you have described as abnormal – and in view of the knowledge you had from various sources that ice was in your immediate vicinity – to proceed at twenty-one and a half knots

Charles Lightoller then all i can say is that recklessness applies to practically every commander and every ship crossing the atlantic ocean

Mr Scanlon i am not disputing that with you – but can you describe it yourself as other than recklessness

Charles Lightoller yes

Mr Scanlon is it careful navigation in your view

Charles Lightoller it is ordinary navigation – which embodies careful navigation

Mr Scanlon is this your position then – that even with the experience of the titanic disaster – if you were coming within the near vicinity of a place which was reported to you to be abounding in ice – would you proceed with a ship like the titanic at twenty-one and a half knots

Charles Lightoller i do not say i should

Mr Scanlon at night and at a time when the conditions were what you have described as very abnormal surely you would not go at twenty-one and a half knots

Charles Lightoller the conditions were not apparent to us in the first place – the conditions of an absolutely flat sea were not apparent to us till afterwards – naturally i should take precautions against such an occurrence

Mr Scanlon and what precautions would you take if you would not slow up or slow down

Charles Lightoller i did not say i would not slow up

Mr Scanlon cannot you say whether you would or not

Charles Lightoller no i am afraid i cannot say right here what i should do – i should take every precaution – whatever appealed to me

Mr Scanlon i suggest to you if you acted carefully and prudently you would slow up – and that if you did not slow up you would be acting recklessly – you know you have described the conditions of abnormality as having been apparent at the time while you were on watch – you have told my lord that at great length – and in your conversations with the captain did you not discuss that – you have said that you did not recognise the sea was flat – i want to recall this to your mind – it is at page 306 my lord question 13615 – you gave this evidence – at five minutes to nine when the commander came on the bridge – i will give it to you as near as i remember – he remarked that it was cold and as far as i remember i said – yes it is very cold sir – in fact i said – it is only one degree above freezing i have sent word down to the carpenter and rung up the engine room and told them that it is freezing or will be during the night – we then commenced to speak about the weather – he said – there is not much wind – i said – no it is a flat calm as a matter of fact – he repeated it – he said – a flat calm – i said – yes quite flat there is no wind – i said something about it was rather a pity the breeze had not kept up whilst we were going through the ice region – of course my reason was obvious he knew i meant the water ripples breaking on the base of the berg

Charles Lightoller yes

Mr Scanlon was not all that amply sufficient to let you and the captain know that you were in circumstances of extreme danger

Charles Lightoller no

Mr Scanlon i do not think anything would convince you that it was dangerous that night

Charles Lightoller i have been very much convinced that it was dangerous

Mr Scanlon i mean that the conditions you have described were dangerous

Charles Lightoller they proved to be

Mr Scanlon what i want to suggest is that the conditions having been so dangerous those in charge of the vessel were negligent in proceeding at that rate of speed

Charles Lightoller no

Mr Scanlon sits.

Clerk the witness withdraws

Joseph Ismay enters.

Clerk days sixteen and seventeen – joseph ismay – managing director of the oceanic steam navigation company and first-class passenger on the titanic – the attorney general

The Attorney General stands.

Attorney General mr ismay you are a member of the firm ismay imrie and company – they are the managers of the oceanic steam navigation company limited

Joseph Ismay yes

Attorney General and that company was the owner of the titanic

Joseph Ismay yes

Attorney General you are also i think managing director of the oceanic steam navigation company limited

Joseph Ismay yes

Attorney General i do not want to go into elaborate detail into the constitution of the company or the american company but i must ask you one or two questions so that my lord may understand how this matter stands – it is a little complicated – but apparently the oceanic steam navigation company limited is an english company is it not

Joseph Ismay yes

Attorney General with its registered office in liverpool

Joseph Ismay with its registered office in liverpool

Attorney General and the oceanic steam navigation company owns all the white star line steamers

Joseph Ismay yes the oceanic steam navigation company is the legal name of the company

Attorney General then there is the mississippi and dominion lines – has that anything to do with the oceanic steam navigation company

Joseph Ismay no

Attorney General that is another

Joseph Ismay it is a separate company altogether

Attorney General that is another company controlled by what i may call for convenience the American shipping trust

Joseph Ismay yes

Attorney General is the international mercantile marine company the name of the american company

Joseph Ismay yes

Attorney General what one speaks of for convenience as the american shipping trust

Joseph Ismay yes

Attorney General i do not mean to suggest that it is a trust – there is some objection i believe in america to calling it a trust – but i only want to get the fact so that we may see where we are about it – that is the american company

Joseph Ismay yes

Attorney General there is one other company which i must refer to – the american shipping trust also controls the leyland line does it not

Joseph Ismay it holds a controlling interest in the leyland line

Commissioner how many lines of steamers does the american trust hold

Joseph Ismay do you mean how many companies my lord or how many different lines

Commissioner i mean how many companies altogether – british companies

Joseph Ismay five i think it is

Commissioner how many american companies does it control

Joseph Ismay two

Commissioner then the american company holds substantially – though not completely – all the share capital in these different companies

Joseph Ismay yes with the exception of the leyland line

Commissioner you told me they had a controlling interest

Joseph Ismay yes there is a controlling interest in the leyland line

Commissioner that is to say they hold the majority of the shares

Attorney General that is it my lord – (*To Witness.*) does the tonnage of these vessels owned or controlled by the american trust in the way you have described represent about a million tons altogether

Joseph Ismay i think it is rather less than a million tons – but very nearly a million tons

Attorney General in round figures it is a million tons

Joseph Ismay yes in round figures it is a million tons

Attorney General but the white star line and these other vessels – which are owned originally by british companies – still run under the british flag do they not

Joseph Ismay yes

Commissioner although these ships – including the titanic – are registered under the british flag they are in fact american property

Joseph Ismay a certain amount of stock in the international maritime company is held in this country but to what extent i have not the slightest idea

Commissioner i should like you to tell me what is the object of an american company managing its affairs through the english laws affecting english companies – why do they do it

Joseph Ismay i am afraid i cannot answer that question my lord

Commissioner i should think you ought to know – you know that in substance the titanic was an american-owned ship

Joseph Ismay that is true

Commissioner in substance – and i want to know why
an american company should manage its ships – or why
it registers its ships – under english management or under
the english flag

Joseph Ismay those ships could not be registered under
the american flag

Commissioner why not

Joseph Ismay because the ships are built i suppose in this
country

Commissioner then according to the laws of america can
no ship that is not american-built be registered there

Joseph Ismay no you cannot register a foreign ship – you
cannot get the american flag for a foreign-built ship – she
must be built in the country

Attorney General will you give me approximately what
the cost of the titanic was

Joseph Ismay a million and a half sterling

Attorney General now – you were on board the titanic
on this voyage

Joseph Ismay i was

Attorney General you sailed in her as a passenger

Joseph Ismay i did

Attorney General she carried mails as well as passengers

Joseph Ismay yes

Attorney General that was under a contract you had
with the british government

Joseph Ismay yes

Attorney General the contract is of course in writing

Joseph Ismay yes

Attorney General can you produce it

Joseph Ismay i have not got it here but it can be produced

Attorney General what i wanted to know was whether there was any such condition in the contract that your vessels must be instructed to steam at twenty knots or anything of that kind

Joseph Ismay that i am not quite clear about – there is some reference in the contract – i think we are allowed to run a ship with mails even at eighteen knots

Attorney General but the substance of it is that you are not bound to proceed at any rate at anything like the speed at which your vessels can go

Joseph Ismay no there is no penalty for not making a certain speed – in other words we get paid a lump sum

Attorney General you were a passenger on the vessel but i suppose you travelled as a passenger because of your interest in the vessel and in the company that owned it

Joseph Ismay naturally i was interested in the ship

Attorney General i mean you had nothing to do in new york – you travelled because you wanted to make the first passage in the titanic

Joseph Ismay partly – but i can always find something to do

Attorney General i mean to say you were not travelling in the titanic because you wanted to go to new york but because you wanted to travel upon the maiden trip of the titanic

Joseph Ismay yes

Attorney General because in your capacity as managing director or as president of the american trust you desired also to see how the vessel behaved i suppose

Joseph Ismay naturally

Attorney General and to see whether anything occurred in the course of the voyage which would lead to suggestions from you or from anybody

Joseph Ismay we were building another new ship and we naturally wanted to see how we could improve on our existing ships

Attorney General that was the real object of your travelling on the titanic

Joseph Ismay and to observe the ship

Attorney General what i want to put to you is that you were not there as an ordinary passenger

Joseph Ismay so far as the navigation of the ship was concerned yes

Attorney General that i will ask you some questions later on about – i am not suggesting that you controlled the navigation – but what i suggest to you is that it would not be right to describe you as really travelling on that ship as an ordinary passenger because of the interest you had in the titanic – and because of your natural watchfulness as to the behaviour of the titanic on her first voyage

Joseph Ismay i looked upon myself simply as an ordinary passenger

Commissioner did you pay your fare

Joseph Ismay no i did not

Attorney General now i think we understand what you mean when you say you were travelling as a passenger –

now on this day – on the 14th – did you get information from the captain of ice reports

Joseph Ismay the captain handed me a marconi message which he had received from the baltic on the sunday

Attorney General he handed you the actual message as it was delivered to him from the baltic

Joseph Ismay yes

Attorney General handed to you because you were the managing director of the company

Joseph Ismay i do not know – it was a matter of information

Attorney General information which he would not give to everybody but which he gave to you – there is not the least doubt about that is there

Joseph Ismay no i do not think so

Attorney General he handed it to you and you read it i suppose

Joseph Ismay yes

Attorney General did he say anything to you about it

Joseph Ismay not a word

Attorney General he merely handed it to you and you put it in your pocket after you read it

Joseph Ismay yes – i glanced at it very casually – i was on the deck at the time

Attorney General had he handed any message to you before this one

Joseph Ismay no

Attorney General so that this was the first message he had handed to you on this voyage

Joseph Ismay yes

Attorney General and when he handed this message to you – when the captain of the ship came to you – the managing director – and put into your hands the marconigram – it was for you to read

Joseph Ismay yes – and i read it

Attorney General and you kept it for the time being

Joseph Ismay yes i put it in my pocket

Attorney General did you understand from the telegram that the ice which was reported was in your track

Joseph Ismay i did not

Attorney General did you attribute any importance at all to the ice report

Joseph Ismay i did not – no special importance at all

Attorney General had you no curiosity to ascertain whether or not you would be travelling in the region in which ice was reported

Joseph Ismay i had not

Attorney General you appreciated that that report meant to you that you were approaching ice

Joseph Ismay yes

Attorney General and you knew also that you would be approaching ice that night

Joseph Ismay i expected so yes

Attorney General and therefore that it behoved those responsible for the navigation of the ship to be very careful

Joseph Ismay naturally

Attorney General and more particularly if you were approaching ice in the night it would be desirable would it not to slow down

Joseph Ismay i am not a navigator

Commissioner answer the question

Joseph Ismay i say no – i am not a navigator

Attorney General you are not quite frank with us mr ismay – you have told me now what your answer is – what was your answer

Joseph Ismay i should say that if a man can see far enough to clear ice he is perfectly justified in going full speed

Attorney General then apparently you did not expect your captain to slow down when he had ice reports

Joseph Ismay no certainly not

Attorney General what is the object of continuing at full speed through the night if you expect to meet ice – why do you do it

Joseph Ismay what is the use of doing it

Attorney General yes

Joseph Ismay i presume that the man would be anxious to get through the ice region – he would not want to slow down upon the chance of a fog coming on

Attorney General so that of course the object of it would be to get through it as fast as you could

Joseph Ismay i presume that if a man on a perfectly clear night could see far enough to clear an iceberg he would be perfectly justified in getting through the ice region as quickly as he possibly could

Attorney General assuming that you can see far enough to get out of the way at whatever speed you are going you can go at whatever speed you like – that is what it comes to

Joseph Ismay assuming you can see far enough to clear the ice

Attorney General i think we understand – now – did you have any conversation with captain smith at all between the time of his giving you the wireless message and the impact with the iceberg about ice

Joseph Ismay the only conversation i had with captain smith was in the smoking room that night – as we walked out of the smoking room he asked me if i had the marconi message and i said yes i had and i gave it to him

Attorney General when the captain asked you for the message and you gave it back to him did you have any conversation with him then

Joseph Ismay no further conversation at all

Attorney General did you not ask him whether your vessel would come at all within that latitude and longitude indicated in the baltic marconigram

Joseph Ismay i did not

Attorney General and he said nothing to you about it

Joseph Ismay he did not

Attorney General now i want to be clear about this – is it your statement to my lord that from first to last on that sunday you never had any conversation with captain smith about ice

Joseph Ismay absolutely

The Attorney General sits.

Mr Scanlon stands.

Mr Scanlon during the voyage had you any conversation with the captain as to speed

Joseph Ismay i had no conversation with the captain with regard to speed or any point of navigation whatever

Mr Scanlon or as to the time of landing

Joseph Ismay or as to the time of landing

Mr Scanlon and you gave him no instructions

Joseph Ismay absolutely none

Mr Scanlon on either of these points

Joseph Ismay no

Mr Scanlon when you had the conversation with reference to speeding up who was present

Joseph Ismay mr bell the chief engineer and my secretary

Mr Scanlon mr bell your secretary and yourself

Joseph Ismay yes

Mr Scanlon what is the name of your secretary

Joseph Ismay mr harrison

Mr Scanlon is he a survivor

Joseph Ismay he is not

Mr Scanlon i think it was decided then that some day in the course of the voyage you would run the ship up to full speed

Joseph Ismay it was

Mr Scanlon and you expected then to take twenty-eight knots out of her

Joseph Ismay i beg your pardon

Mr Scanlon you expected then that she would do seventy-eight revolutions

Joseph Ismay yes

Mr Scanlon now mr ismay i want to ask you this question – what right had you – as an ordinary passenger – to decide the speed the ship was to go at without consultation with the captain

Commissioner well i can answer that – none – you are asking him something that is quite obvious – he has no right to dictate what the speed is to be

Mr Scanlon but he may as a super captain

Commissioner what sort of a person is a super captain

Mr Scanlon i will tell you as i conceive it my lord – it is a man like mr ismay who can say to the chief engineer of a ship what speed the ship is to run at

Commissioner i do not know that he did – you know the captain is the man who must say all those things

Mr Scanlon i daresay my lord – but i think it is important that this conversation and this decision was not arrived at – with regard to the speed of the ship – in the presence of the captain – but was arrived at at a meeting between this gentleman and the chief engineer

Commissioner i suppose the captain would or ought to know hour by hour what his ship is steaming

Mr Scanlon i should think my lord

Commissioner never mind we will not argue about it – the question you put to him is answered by me – you take my answer that he had no right at all to do anything of the kind

Mr Scanlon i will take it that that would be his answer my lord

Commissioner i do not know whether it would

Mr Scanlon sits.

Mr Harbinson stands.

Mr Harbinson you told my lord about this telegram that captain smith showed to you on the afternoon of sunday the 14th

Joseph Ismay yes

Mr Harbinson as a matter of fact you had discussed this question of speed with mr bell in queenstown – now would i be stating what was accurate if i said you were more or less partly responsible for the speed the titanic was making going across the atlantic

Joseph Ismay i was not responsible for the speed of the ship in any degree

Commissioner that is not a question to put to him

Mr Harbinson i will put it to him in this way if i may – (*To Witness.*) did you say in america on the first day of proceedings – it was our intention if we had fine weather on monday afternoon or tuesday to drive the ship at full speed – you say there – it was our intention – you mean i presume it was the intention of yourself and the captain

Joseph Ismay it was the intention to run the ship for about four hours at full speed

Mr Harbinson you say it was our intention – it was the intention

Joseph Ismay yes

Mr Harbinson i suggest to you you were one of those responsible for controlling the speed and generally directing it

Joseph Ismay no i was not

Commissioner oh no – he was not responsible – and he had no business to interfere in such matters

Mr Harbinson perhaps i would be more accurate if i put it this way

Commissioner what i think you want to suggest is that he took upon himself to ask that it should be done – apparently he did

Mr Harbinson it was his influence that was responsible for it – perhaps not actively carrying it out – but he instigated it – (*To Witness.*) you used the word our there you notice

Joseph Ismay it was the intention

Mr Harbinson and you say this further on page 3 in answer to a question – the question was put – you spoke of the revolutions on the early part of the voyage – answer – yes sir – question – those were increased as the distance was increased – answer – the titanic being a new ship we were gradually working her up – you see you use the same personal pronoun – we – incorporating yourself

Joseph Ismay i could not say i was gradually working her up

Mr Harbinson you could have said – the captain

Joseph Ismay i daresay i could

Mr Harbinson you said – we

Joseph Ismay perhaps i should've said – she was being gradually worked up

Commissioner i have often been on these steamers or similar steamers and i have said to another passenger – we are doing so many miles a day – but i never imagined i was interfering in the navigation or was responsible for it

Mr Harbinson no my lord – i should think your lordship is much too good a maritime lawyer to ever dream of doing so – (*To Witness.*) there is one suggestion i should very much like to make to you mr ismay and it is this – it did strike you as rather an exceptional thing – the captain showing you this marconigram with regard to the ice – the message that he received from the baltic

Joseph Ismay no it was not an exceptional thing

Mr Harbinson i suggest to you that the captain in doing so – in showing this marconigram to you – the managing director – was inviting an expression of opinion from you on the question of the speed that the vessel should take

Commissioner really you must not ask such a question – ask about facts – and then when you come if you ever do come – i do not know we shall ever reach it – to the time when you make a speech – then you can make these suggestions to me – but at present confine yourself to asking the witness about facts – have you any other questions

Mr Harbinson no my lord i think not

Mr Harbinson sits.

Clerk the witness withdraws

Sir Ernest Shackleton enters.

Clerk day twenty-six – sir ernest shackleton – explorer – the attorney general

The Attorney General stands.

Attorney General you have had a large experience of ice

Sir Ernest Shackleton yes

Attorney General i want you to help the court with your views as a result of your experience – first of all with regard to the visibility of ice in clear weather – take icebergs first

Sir Ernest Shackleton that entirely depends on the height of the iceberg – take an iceberg of about eighty feet high and the ordinary type that has not turned over yet – you could see that in clear weather about ten or twelve miles

Attorney General at night

Sir Ernest Shackleton not at night no – i would say provided it was an ordinary berg about five miles on a clear night

Commissioner at night

Sir Ernest Shackleton yes at night

Attorney General you said provided it was an ordinary berg

Sir Ernest Shackleton yes

Attorney General are there bergs that present a different appearance in colour

Sir Ernest Shackleton there are many bergs i have seen that appear to be black due to the construction of the berg itself – and also due to the earthy matter and rocks that are in all bergs – after a berg has capsized if it is not of close construction it is more porous and taking up the water does not reflect light in any way

Attorney General have you had large experience of this particular track

Sir Ernest Shackleton not much – only four or five times i have seen ice in the north atlantic

Attorney General have you ever seen ice of this particular dark character to which you have referred in the north atlantic

Sir Ernest Shackleton yes twice

Commissioner in the north atlantic

Sir Ernest Shackleton yes

Attorney General how far would you see one of these dark bergs on a clear night assuming it to be sixty to eighty feet high

Sir Ernest Shackleton it might be only three miles depending on the night and depending almost entirely on the condition of the sea at the time – with a dead calm sea there is no sign at all to give you any indication that there is anything there – if you first see the breaking sea at all then you look for the rest and you generally see it – that is on the waterline – i do not say very high because from a height it is not so easily seen – it blends with the ocean if you are looking down at an angle like that – if you are on the sea level it may loom up

Attorney General that would rather suggest that your view would be that you could detect bergs of that kind better at the stem than you could at the crow's nest

Sir Ernest Shackleton better the nearer you are to the waterline – when we navigated in thick or hazy weather there was always one man on the lookout and one man as near the deck line as possible

Attorney General and supposing you were passing through a zone where you had ice reported to you would you take precautions as to the lookout – supposing you only had men in the crow's nest would you take any other precautions

Sir Ernest Shackleton i would take the ordinary precaution of slowing down whether i was in a ship equipped for ice or any other – compatible with keeping steerage way for the size of the ship

Attorney General you would slow down

Sir Ernest Shackleton i would slow down yes

Attorney General and supposing you were going twenty-one to twenty-two knots – i suppose that would be the better reason for slowing down

Sir Ernest Shackleton you have no right to go at that speed in an ice zone

Commissioner and you think that all these liners are wrong in going at this speed in regions where ice has been reported

Sir Ernest Shackleton where it has been reported i think the possibility of accident is greatly enhanced by the speed the ship goes

Commissioner we have been told that none of these liners slow down even though they know that they are going through an ice region – that is to say a region where there are icebergs

Sir Ernest Shackleton i have been in a ship which was specifically built for ice but i took the precaution to slow down because you can only tell the condition of any ice you see – there may be projecting spurs and you may suddenly come across them

Attorney General i still want you to give me your attention with regard to the lookout – you have told me your views with regard to speed – suppose you had two men in the crow's nest and it was a clear night and you were going through a region in which ice had been reported – would you put any person in the bow for a lookout

Sir Ernest Shackleton i would put a lookout man in the bow or as near to the waterline as possible – even on a clear night – but i would only use one man in the crow's nest

Attorney General your idea would be that of the two men – when coming into an ice region – one should go to the bow and one should be in the crow's nest

Sir Ernest Shackleton my main reason for saying one man in the crow's nest is that i think one man gives more attention to the work in hand than two men

Attorney General there is a good deal to be said for that

Commissioner yes i think so

Attorney General one other matter i wanted you to tell us about and that is with regard to the use of glasses for the lookout men – you know the point – it has been suggested here that binoculars should be used by the lookout men particularly if they have had a report of ice – will you tell my lord your view about that

Sir Ernest Shackleton my lord i do not believe in any lookout man having glasses at all – i only believe in the officer using them and then only when something has been reported in a certain quarter or a certain place in the bow

Attorney General the man would pick it up with his eyes and the officer would find out what it is with the glasses

Sir Ernest Shackleton yes – you have the whole range of the horizon in one moment with your eyes and you localise it by using glasses

Attorney General i ought to ask you this – is there any indication of the proximity of ice by the fall of temperature

Sir Ernest Shackleton unless the wind is blowing from a large field of ice to windward there is no indication at all by the methods that are used now – and it is a very poor thing to go upon – is the change of temperature – the film of fresh water that covers the sea is so thin that by dipping in a bucket you do not pick up that thin cold water – and if the temperature of the air is approximately

the temperature of the sea there is practically no haze –
it is only when the water is warmer or the air is warmer
that the haze occurs – there are no methods that i have
heard of before this that can really give you an indication
of approaching ice by ordinary temperature methods

Commissioner we have been told that on this night the
conditions were very peculiar and the sea was as flat as a
table top and that there was no sort of swell – and
therefore nothing that would make a ridge round the
waterline of the iceberg on which the eye would fall – we
have been told that this iceberg was black and it has been
said that in those circumstances it is very difficult to detect
the existence of a berg in time to avoid it – is that so

Sir Ernest Shackleton i agree with that my lord – i think
it would have been a very difficult thing with a ship going
at that speed to have done so

Commissioner do you think the speed makes any
difference in picking up a thing

Sir Ernest Shackleton i do not know about picking up
but slower speed gives you a longer time from the time
you see it at the same distance

Commissioner what would you say would be the shortest
distance that this berg would be seen by the men in the
crow's nest on a clear night

Sir Ernest Shackleton the shortest distance from the ship

Commissioner yes on a perfectly clear night and under
these conditions of a flat sea and possibly black ice

Sir Ernest Shackleton i would not like to express an
opinion because i have never actually seen a berg as close
to a ship – i have never seen any ice quite exactly like that
which was described – i have seen it in the wintertime in
the ice – but then we were always absolutely stationary

Commissioner my difficulty is this – and i am afraid you cannot help me – but i cannot understand how the men in the crow's nest and the men on the bridge – there were two i think – one at all events on the bridge – failed to see this iceberg until it was practically in contact with the ship

Sir Ernest Shackleton i think that iceberg was such a very little thing – it was such a small thing and the conditions were so bad that a man on watch – even two hours on watch – might have his eyes strained and the officer on watch might have his eyes strained and might just miss that particular berg – in running round the horizon his eyes might hop over this particular thing

Commissioner but there were three pairs of eyes – there was a man on the bridge and two in the crow's nest

Sir Ernest Shackleton i think that is a possibility

Commissioner is it a probability

Sir Ernest Shackleton i think it is a probability – i think they might not see such a thing

Commissioner then do you really mean to say that on a fine night with a flat sea the probable thing is that every ship will come in contact with an iceberg that happens to be on its course

Sir Ernest Shackleton no my lord i think it is an abnormal case entirely

Commissioner i am putting an abnormal case – an extraordinarily flat sea and black ice – do you think if there happens to be an iceberg in the course of that ship she must run up against it – although there are three men on watch

Sir Ernest Shackleton the next time somebody may see it a little earlier – it is possible to see it a little earlier but i do not like to express an opinion

Commissioner you said the probability was the ship would run up against the iceberg

Attorney General your lordship will remember she is going seven hundred yards a minute and it would not take long

Commissioner i know that – (*To Witness.*) i want to know this – do these bergs extend sometimes under the water any considerable distance from the part that is visible

Sir Ernest Shackleton it depends – if the berg is capsized it may extend perhaps two hundred yards or more depending on the size of the berg – some bergs that are five miles long – which is rarely seen in the atlantic – may extend two or three hundred yards – what we call a spur – but not more than that

Commissioner so that the bottom of the ship might strike an iceberg before it reached what you may call the locality of the part that is uppermost

Sir Ernest Shackleton yes before it actually struck the part above the water

Commissioner but you think in an extreme case only two hundred yards

Sir Ernest Shackleton yes an extreme case

Commissioner did you say two hundred yards

Sir Ernest Shackleton i have seen spurs two hundred yards away – but i think a couple of hundred feet would be about the average for a spur – a lot depends upon the sort of ice – what sort of mountain it came off – and what its specific gravity is – whether it is worn down in the current by the temperature of the water

Commissioner but the bottom of the berg may extend under the water any distance from two hundred feet to six hundred feet

Sir Ernest Shackleton yes

Commissioner away from the visible berg itself

Sir Ernest Shackleton away from the visible vertical side of the berg

Commissioner so that the bottom of the ship might strike a berg any distance from two hundred to six hundred feet away from the berg

Sir Ernest Shackleton yes that is my opinion my lord – there are no doubt other people who have also got perhaps slightly different opinions – but in the main – generalising – it is so

Commissioner i rather gather from what you have said to me – i am not sure that i ought to ask you this question but i am going to ask it all the same – that you think it quite possible that the men were keeping as good a lookout as they could

Sir Ernest Shackleton yes that is what i do think

Commissioner there is another question i am not sure i ought to ask you – supposing it had been the invariable practice to navigate ships of this kind – following the usual track to america – at full speed – notwithstanding ice warnings – in your opinion would a captain who had been brought up in that trade be justified in following the practice – now do not answer that question if you do not like – if you have not formed any opinion about it i will not press you to give an answer

Sir Ernest Shackleton we sailors all form opinions my lord like other people – but it opens up such a very wide question of relationship between owners and captains that i am not competent to answer it – i think it would be a natural thing for a captain who has been brought up in a line doing the same thing to continue doing it – but in view of the fact that there is wireless yes i think any accident could be avoided

The lights begin to fade on the courtroom.

Clerk scenes from the british wreck commissioner's inquiry 1912 – (*Reads from a page.*) the following were the numbers saved – first class – adult males – 57 out of 175 – adult females – 140 out of 144 – male children – 5 all saved – female children – 1 all saved – in total 203 out of 325 saved – second class – adult males – 14 out of 168 – adult females – 80 out of 93 – male children – 11 all saved – female children – 13 all saved – in total 118 out of 285 saved – third class – adult males – 75 out of 462 – adult females – 76 out of 165 – male children – 13 out of 48 – female children – 14 out of 31 – in total 178 out of 706 – crew saved – deck department – 43 out of 66 – engine room department – 72 out of 325 – victualling department – 97 out of 494 – in total – both passengers and crew – 711 out of 2201 – and now for the dead – (*Reading from another page.*) senator william alden smith said during his address to the senate in delivering the titanic panel's report on may 28th 1912 – in our imagination we can see again the proud ship instinct with life and energy with active figures again swarming upon its decks – musicians teachers artists and authors – soldiers and sailors and men of large affairs – brave men and noble women of every land – we can see the unpretentious and the lowly – progenitors of the great and the strong – turning their back upon the old world where endurance is to them no longer a virtue and looking hopefully to the new – at the very moment of their greatest joy the ship suddenly reels – mutilated and groaning – with splendid courage the musicians fill the last moments with sympathetic melody – the ship wearily gives up the unequal battle – only a vestige remains of the men and women that but a moment before quickened her

spacious apartments with human hopes and passions –
sorrows and joys – upon that broken hull new vows were
taken – new fealty expressed – old love renewed – and
those who had been devoted in friendship and companions
in life went proudly and defiantly on the last pilgrimage
together – in such a heritage we must feel ourselves more
intimately related to the sea than ever before – and
henceforth it will send back to us on its rising tide the
cheering salutations from those we have lost . . .

Lights fade to dark.